Pictures

This is a **picture/ a photo, a sketch,
an aerial photograph, a drawing, a cartoon**, showing ...
Something ... is located
    in the foreground.
    in the middle / in the centre.
    in the background.
    in the top left corner.
    in the bottom left corner.
    in the left-hand corner.
    in the right-hand corner.

This **photo shows** *a desert*.
This is a **photo of** *the Sahara desert*.

The **photo**
    was taken **in** ...
    was taken **at** ...
    was taken **on** ...

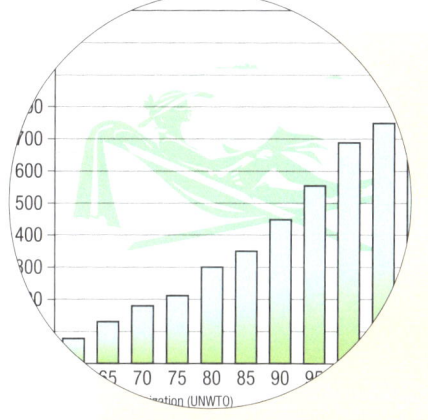

Graphs

The **title of this graph is** about *the development of tourism*.
This **bar / line graph is about** *the development of the number of tourists* **from** (*1960*) **to** (*2012*).
The number of tourists **rises / falls from** ... **to** ...
The **bars show / indicate the number of** (*people*).

The **labels show the units of the x-axis / y-axis**.
The **amount / amounts of** ... **is / are given in** ...
The **bars help to compare the amount of** ...
This **bar graph shows** (the size of continents).

The **climate graph shows the climate of** ...
The **temperature rises from 15 to 20 degrees Celsius (°C) / Fahrenheit (°F).**
The **temperature falls from 20 to 15 degrees Celsius (°C) / Fahrenheit (°F).**
The **warmest / coolest month is** (August).
The **precipitation is highest / lowest in** (July).

Diercke Geography

For Bilingual Classes

Basic

Moderation:
Prof. Dr. Reinhard Hoffmann

Autorinnen und Autoren:
Verena Hundertmark
Dorothee Klein
Dirk Reischauer
Ingo Warken
unter Mitwirkung der Verlagsredaktion

westermann

Cover: Tower Bridge (London, UK)

Mit Beiträgen von:
Matthew Appleby †, Brigitte Dreymüller,
Volker Friedrich, Dieter Haupt, Dimo M. Rischke,
Horst Weible

CARL DIERCKE (geb. in Kyritz, Landkreis Ostprignitz/Preußen) lebte von 1842 bis 1913 und war Pädagoge und Kartograph. Von ihm stammt der bekannte *Diercke-Schulatlas*, der erstmals 1883 unter dem Namen „*Schul-Atlas über alle Teile der Erde*" erschien. Weitere Informationen können dem Internet entnommen werden: *www.diercke.de – (Info/Chronik)*

© 2017 Bildungshaus Schulbuchverlage Westermann Schroedel Diesterweg Schöningh Winklers GmbH, Georg-Westermann-Allee 66, 38104 Braunschweig
www.westermann.de

Das Werk und seine Teile sind urheberrechtlich geschützt. Jede Nutzung in anderen als den gesetzlich zugelassenen bzw. vertraglich zugestandenen Fällen bedarf der vorherigen schriftlichen Einwilligung des Verlages. Nähere Informationen zur vertraglich gestatteten Anzahl von Kopien finden Sie auf www.schulbuchkopie.de.

Für Verweise (Links) auf Internet-Adressen gilt folgender Haftungshinweis: Trotz sorgfältiger inhaltlicher Kontrolle wird die Haftung für die Inhalte der externen Seiten ausgeschlossen. Für den Inhalt dieser externen Seiten sind ausschließlich deren Betreiber verantwortlich. Sollten Sie daher auf kostenpflichtige, illegale oder anstößige Inhalte treffen, so bedauern wir dies ausdrücklich und bitten Sie, uns umgehend per E-Mail davon in Kenntnis zu setzen, damit beim Nachdruck der Verweis gelöscht wird.

Druck A^6 / Jahr 2023
Alle Drucke der Serie A sind im Unterricht parallel verwendbar.

Redaktion: Lars Büttner
Bildredaktion: Susanne Guse
Umschlaggestaltung: Thomas Schröder
Druck und Bindung: Westermann Druck GmbH, Georg-Westermann-Allee 66, 38104 Braunschweig

ISBN 978-3-14-**114030**-9

Zur Arbeit mit diesem Buch

Rubriken

 - Information:
Hier werden Begriffe oder Zusammenhänge kurz erläutert.

FACT SHEET - Steckbrief:
Faktensammlung zu einer Region.

KEY TERMS - Fachbegriffe:
Diese Begriffe solltest du kennen! Für sie wurde daher am Ende des Buches ein Lexikon (Glossary) eingerichtet.

STEPS - Arbeitsschritte:
Hier sind die Arbeitsschritte für eine Methode übersichtlich aufgelistet.

TASKS - Aufgaben:
Die Aufgaben helfen dir, das Gelernte zu üben, zu vertiefen oder zu erweitern. For experts: Diese Aufgaben sind schwieriger und erfordern einen höheren Arbeitsaufwand.

Verweise
- auf das Internet:
- auf Methodenseiten (Geo Skills):
- auf Themenseiten: (› pp 14-15)
- auf Materialien: (**M** + Nummer)

Atlashinweise
Schlage den Atlas auf der angegebenen Seite auf oder gib den Karten-Code im Suchfeld der Internet-Adresse ein:

Blaues Symbol:
Diercke Weltatlas

Gelbes Symbol:
Diercke International Atlas

Contents

4 The World We Live in

- 6 Our Solar System
- 8 Geography – Our New Subject
- 10 Continents and Oceans
- 12 7,000,000,000 People
- 14 Day and Night
- 16 The Global Grid
- 18 Time Zones
- 20 Reasons for Seasons
- 22 What is Weather?
- 24 How We Can Measure and Record ...
- 26 Different Landscapes

28 Germany and Europe

- 30 The Federal Republic of Germany
- 32 What Do Germany's Landscapes Look Like?
- 34 Discover Europe
- 36 Living Together in Europe
- 38 European Climatic Regions
- 40 Agriculture in Great Britain
- 42 An Arable Farm in Essex
- 44 Oil and Gas – Non-renewable Resources from the North Sea
- 46 Renewable Energy
- 48 Industries in the London Area
- 50 A European Aeroplane for the World
- 52 A Working Day in Edinburgh
- 54 Living in Edinburgh
- 56 The Many Sides of Tourism
- 58 Holidays in the Alps
- 60 Malta – A Famous Tourist Place

62 Geo Skills

- 62 How to Work with the Atlas
- 64 How to Read Maps
- 66 How to Work with Climate Graphs

68 Appendix

- 68 Tasks – Knowing What to Do
- 70 Words
- 74 Glossary

The World We Live in

6	Our Solar System
8	Geography – Our New Subject
10	Continents and Oceans
12	7,000,000,000 People
14	Day and Night
16	The Global Grid
18	Time Zones
20	Reasons for Seasons
22	What is Weather?
24	How We Can Measure and Record ...
26	Different Landscapes

M1 Earth and Moon in space

Our Solar System

In the middle of our solar system is the Sun. Eight planets orbit the Sun. Our Earth is one of the planets. One trip of the Earth around the Sun takes one year.
Moons orbit most planets, the Earth has got only one moon.

Sun   Mercury   Venus   Earth   Mars

Jupiter

	Diameter (km)	Number of moons	Orbit around Sun
Sun	1,392,700	–	–
Jupiter	142,984	67	11.9 years
Saturn	120,536	62	29.5 years
Uranus	51,118	27	84.0 years
Neptune	49,520	14	164.8 years
Earth	12,756	1	365.3 days = 1 year
Venus	12,104	0	224.7 days = 0.6 years
Mars	6,787	2	687.0 days = 1.9 years
Mercury	4,878	0	88.0 days = 0.2 years

M1 Sun, Earth and the other planets (2014)

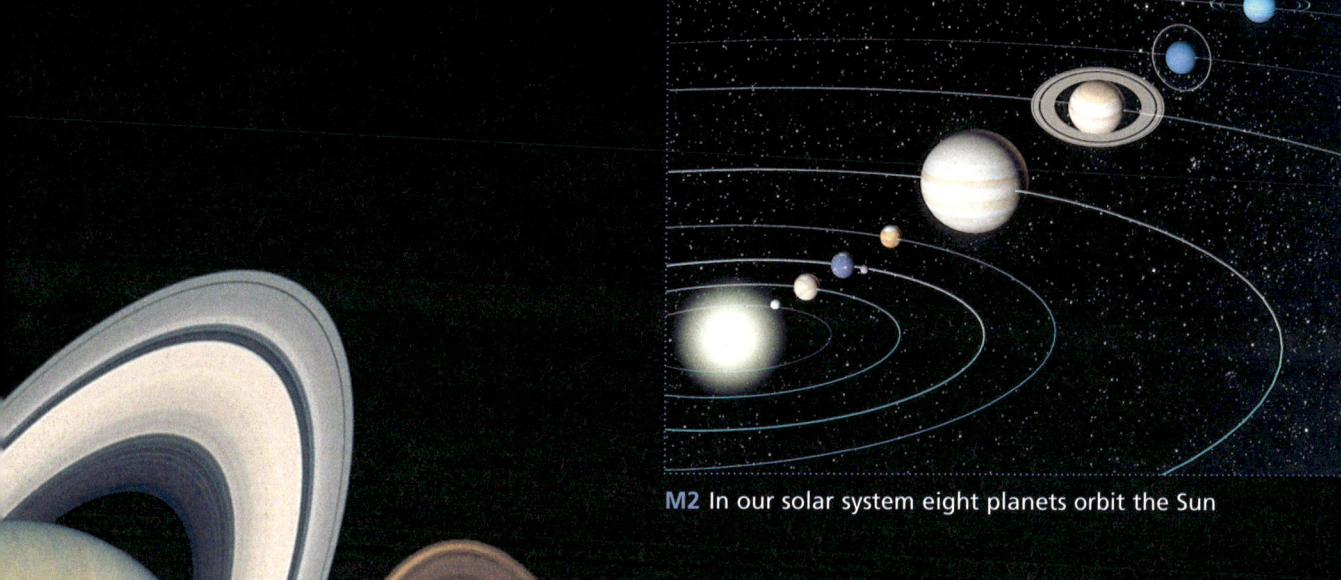

M2 In our solar system eight planets orbit the Sun

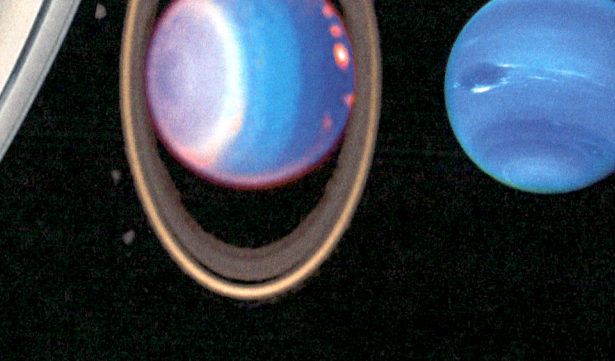

Saturn   Uranus   Neptune

TASKS

① This is an example of a sentence to remember the order of the planets from the Sun:
My Very Easy Method Just Speeds Up Names.
Make your own German sentence!

② Compare the Sun with the planets (M1).

KEY TERMS

- Earth
- moon
- planet
- solar system
- Sun

HELPFUL WORDS AND PHRASES

for TASK 2:
- ... orbits the Sun in ... years / days.
- One trip around the Sun takes ...
- This is shorter / longer than ...
- ... has got ... moon(s).
- This is more / less than ...
- ... is smaller / bigger than ...

Geography – Our New Subject

M1 Rock climbing in the Alps

Geography brings you to the world around us. It is about how people live around the world. A Geographer wants to find out where something is and why it is there. Geographers look at nature to find out how it affects people's lives, for example: Where is it cold or warm on Earth? Where can plants grow? Why is there rain in some places and not in other places?

Geography is also about how people's lives are different in different places, for example: How do they live in cities and villages? What jobs do they do? How do they travel or what do they do in their free time?

People change nature with their actions. So Geographers want to find out how people do this.

Geography
Geography comes from two Greek words:
Geos = Earth
and
graphein = to describe

TASKS

1. Describe the photo. Use the given words.
2. Make two lists: Which words in the photo are about people? Which words are about nature?
3. Describe what Geography is about. Use the lists and the text.
4. Point out in English or German what makes Geography interesting for you.

HELPFUL WORDS AND PHRASES

for TASK 1:
- I can see …
- There is / are …
- In the background / foreground …
- On the left / right …

for TASK 4:
- I like Geography because …
- I want to know more about …

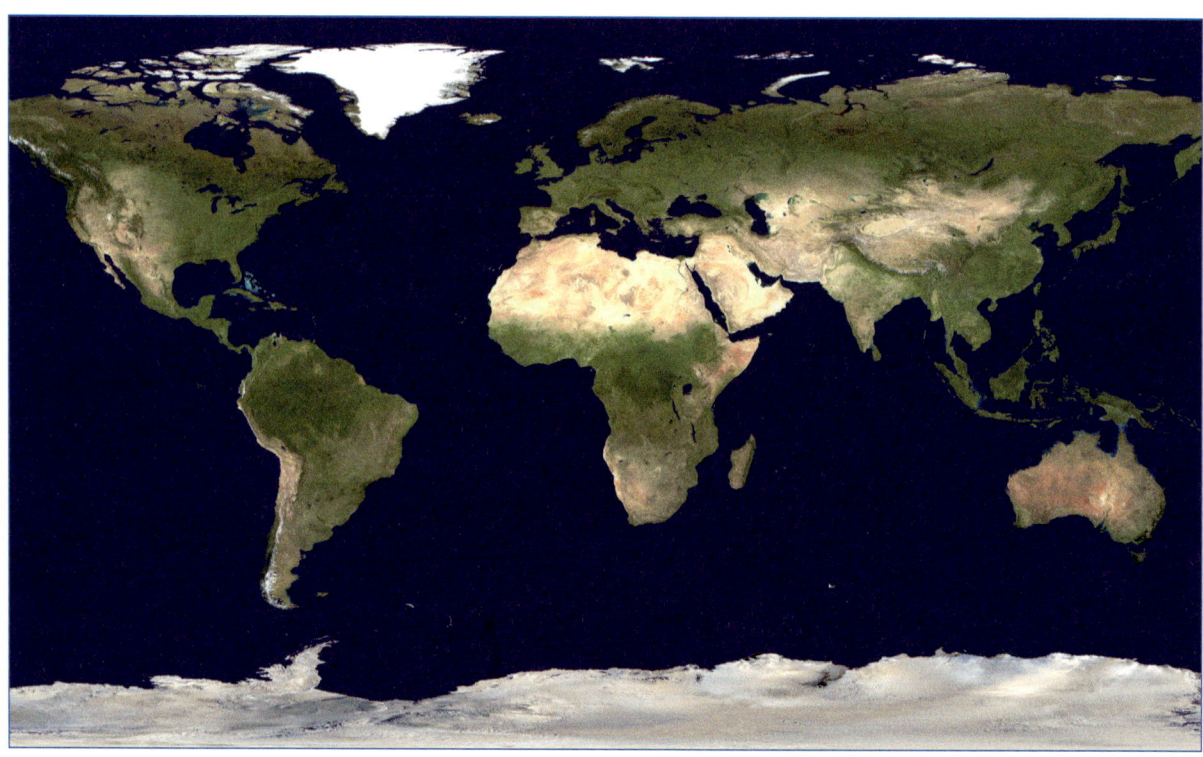

M1 Satellite image of the Earth

Continents and Oceans

We live on a planet of continents and oceans. Continents are large landmasses. There are seven continents: Europe, Asia, Australia, Africa, North America, South America, and Antarctica.
Most landmasses are north of the Equator, in the Northern Hemisphere (> p. 17).

Water is all around these landmasses. We call these large areas of water oceans. There are three oceans on our planet: the Pacific, the Atlantic, and the Indian Ocean. Although we give different names to the oceans, they are in fact only one big body of water.

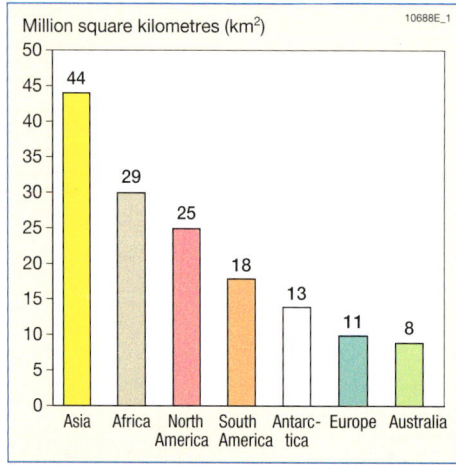

M2 Sizes of the continents

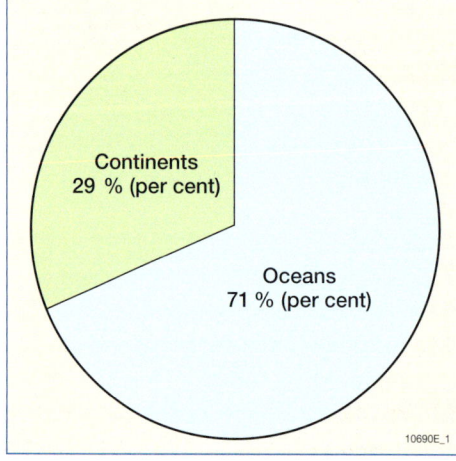

M3 Land and water on Earth

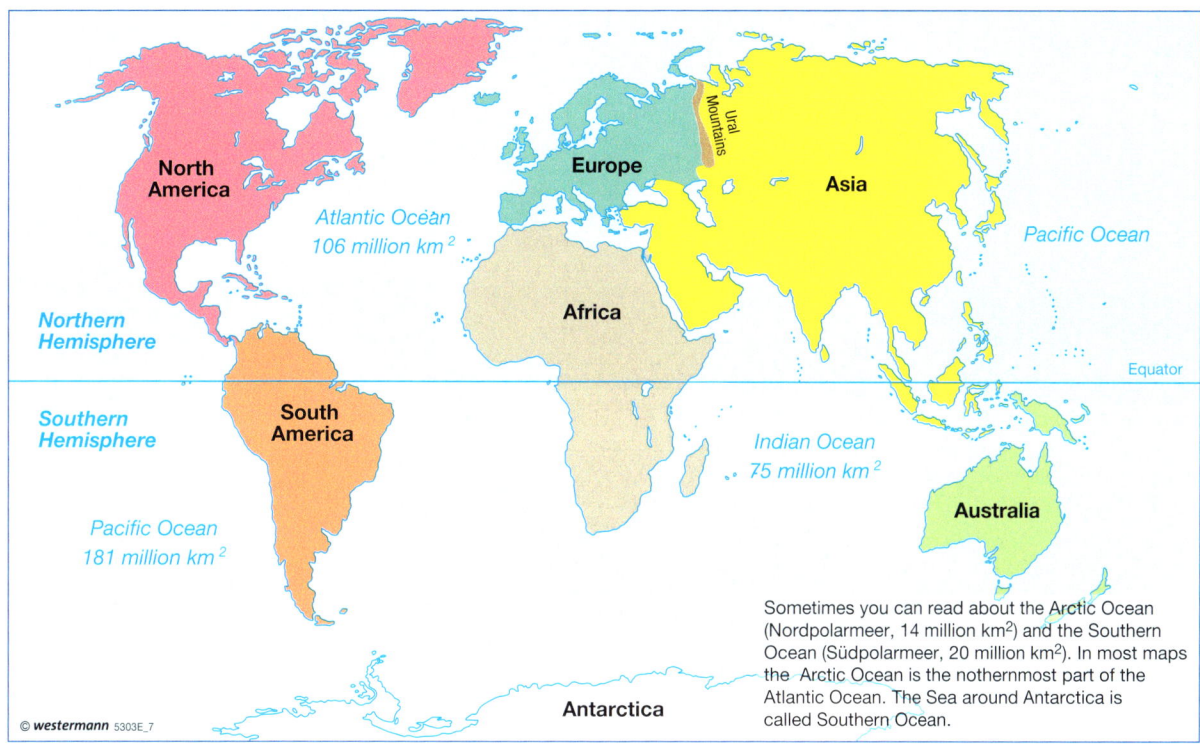

M4 Continents and oceans

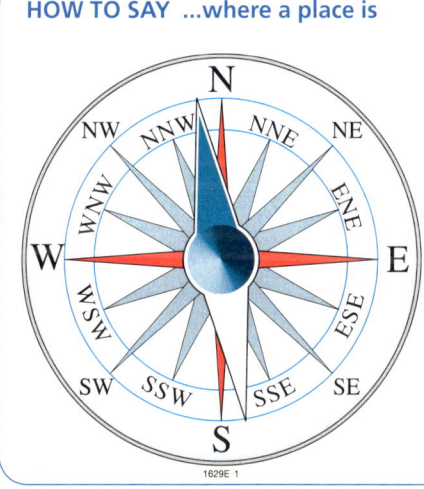

HOW TO SAY ...where a place is

North, south, east and west are the points of the compass.
With the help of the points of the compass we can give directions. Here are some examples of how you can say where a place is:

- 'Place A lies north / south / west / east of place B.'
- 'Place A is located / is situated north / northeast / southwest / west-northwest ... of place B.'

M5 Points of the compass

HELPFUL WORDS AND PHRASES

for TASK 2:
- ... lies between ... and ...
- ... lies north / south / west / east of ...

for TASK 3:
- ... is bigger than ...
- ... is smaller than ...
- ... is as big as ...
- ... is the biggest ...
- ... is the smallest ...
- There is more ... than ...

TASKS

1. Name the continents and oceans in English and German.
2. Describe the position of the continents and oceans with the help of **M4** and **M5**.
3. Compare the sizes of the continents with the help of **M2**.
4. Draw a bar graph of the sizes of the oceans (**M4**).

KEY TERMS

- body of water
- continent
- landmass
- ocean
- points of the compass

7,000,000,000 People

The Earth has got more than 7,000,000,000 inhabitants. They live permanently on all continents, except Antarctica. Some countries have a high population, others only have a small one. People speak different

'My name is Alice. I live in Dawson, Canada. I do lots of things in my free time. In summer I go fly-fishing or swimming with my friends. But in winter it's not so easy. It snows a lot. So skiing is my favourite winter hobby.'

M1 Living in Canada

'I'm Raul from Rio de Janeiro, Brazil. I live in a Bungalow park. There is a wall around the park, so nobody can come in. Our house is very big: my brothers and I have our own rooms. We have a swimming pool and a garden.'

M2 Living in Brazil

'Hi! I'm Asale from Malawi. I live in a small village in the savanna. My family and I make our own food: we grow crops on fields and get meat from our cows. Some of the crops we grow on the fields are: manioc, millet and maize.'

M3 Living in Malawi

 www.worldometers.info

 D1-252 www.diercke.de

 DE-190 www.diercke.com

languages, have different religions and live in cities, in villages or sometimes they do not even have a home. They buy their food in different places: on markets, in shops or in the street. Schools are different, too.

■ Countries with more than 1 billion inhabitants

● Countries with more than 100 million inhabitants

M4 Countries with a high population

'My name is Rohit and I live in Mumbai, India. It's a very big city with millions of inhabitants. The trains are so crowded that people even sit on the roofs. I love to use my bicycle, but there are many cars, motorcycles, rickshaws and even carts with donkeys.'

M5 Living in India

'Howdy! I'm Mary from Tasmania, Australia. I go to Devonport High School. Our school day is very long, so we have lunch in the cafeteria. My favourite subject is Maths. But I also like Health and Art. We use the computer a lot in our lessons.'

M6 Living in Australia

TASKS

1. Make a list: What do the children talk about?
2. Write a text about yourself: How do you live?
3. Compare your life to the children's lives.

KEY TERMS

- inhabitant
- language
- population
- religion

HELPFUL WORDS AND PHRASES

for TASK 3:
- I go to school by bus / train / bike ...
- I go to school on foot ...
- In my school we ...
- This is better / worse ...
- I spend more / less time on ...

Day and Night

Like the other planets, the Earth spins on its axis. This is an invisible line between the North Pole and the South Pole. The upper end of this axis is the North Pole. The axis has got a tilt, so the North Pole and the South Pole are not straight up and down (**M1**). A globe is a model of the Earth. We can see the continents, oceans, seas and islands. With a globe you can show how the Earth spins on its axis (**M3**).

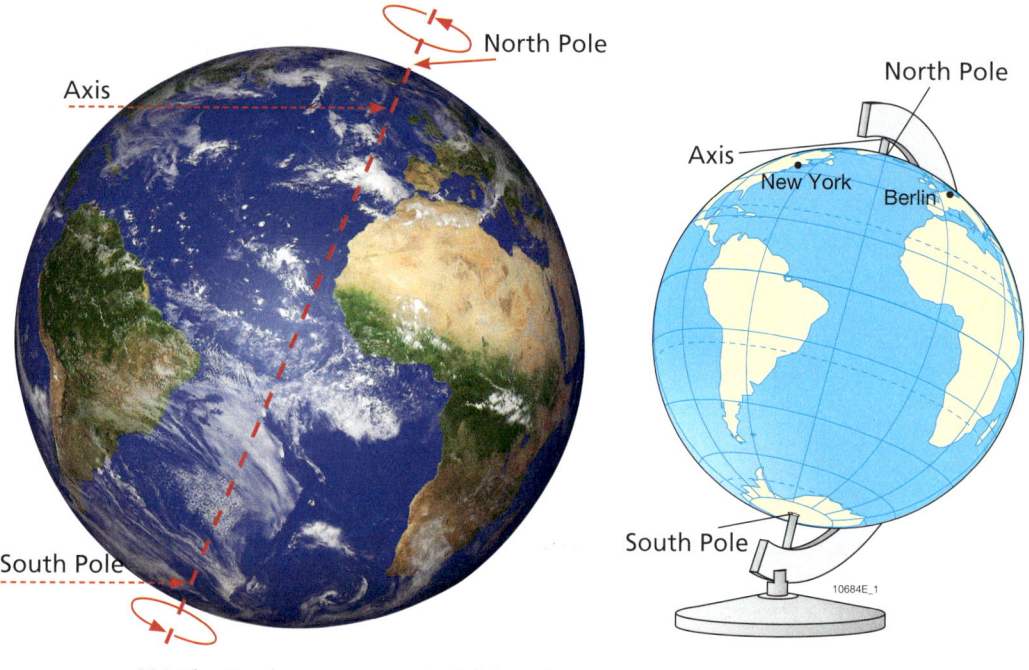

M1 The Earth turns on an invisible axis

M3 A globe

M2 A day in Berlin

Day and night on Earth

The Earth spins on its axis once every 24 hours from west to east. This spinning causes day and night as the Sun only shines on one half of the Earth.
The part of the Earth away from the Sun is in darkness, so it has got nighttime, the other side has got daytime.

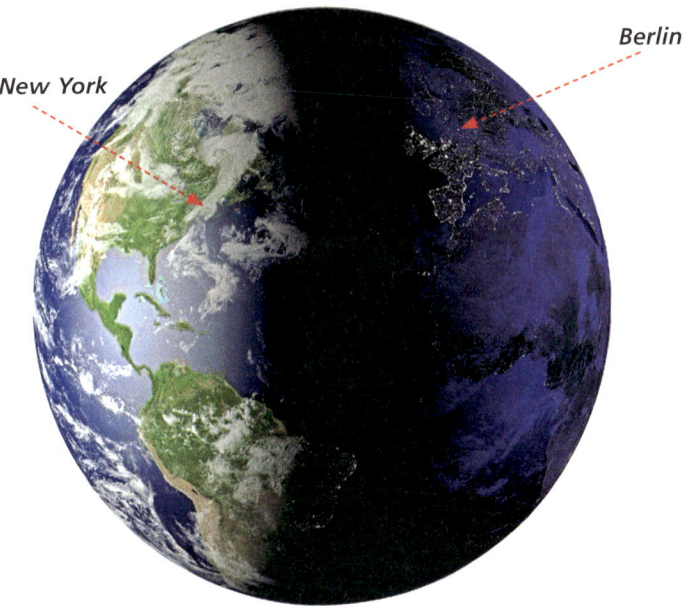

M4 Daytime and nighttime on Earth

TASKS

1. Write short German definitions of the following terms: North Pole – South Pole – tilted axis – globe. Use **M1**, **M3** and the text.
2. Set up an experiment to show how day and night come about. Use a globe and a torch.
3. Explain day and night with the help of **M1**, **M2**, and your experiment.

KEY TERMS

- axis
- daytime
- globe
- nighttime
- North Pole
- South Pole
- tilt

HELPFUL WORDS AND PHRASES
for TASK 3:
- The Earth spins …
- When the Sun shines on …, the other side of the Earth is …

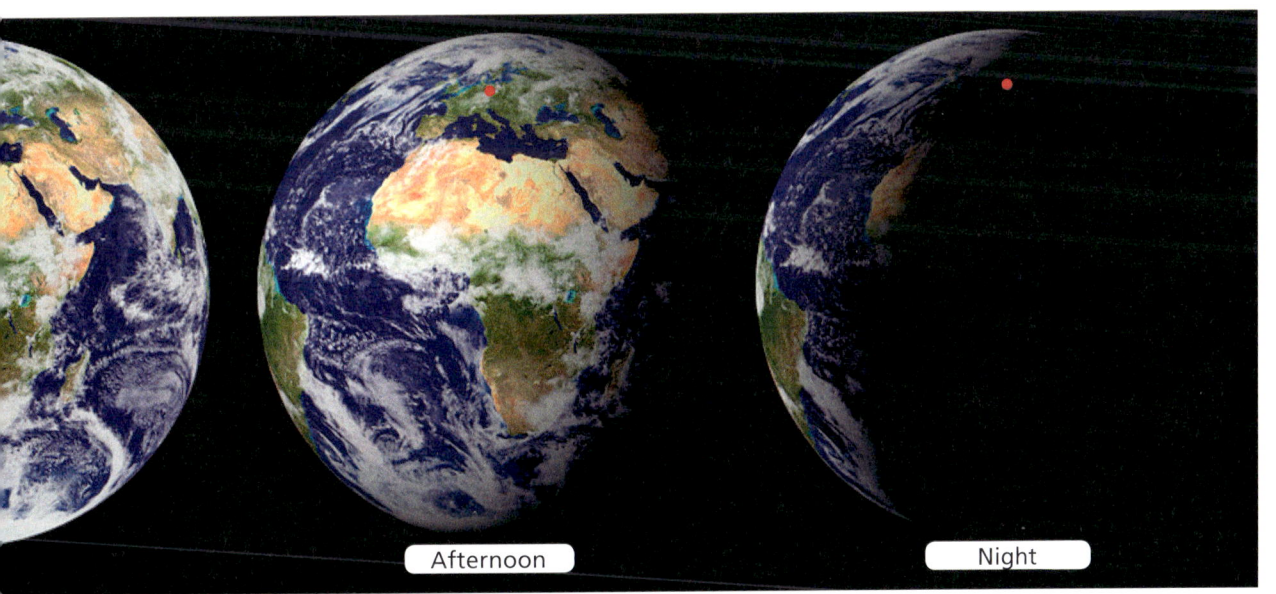

Afternoon   Night

M1 Modern treasure hunters

The Global Grid

Modern treasure hunters

Today, treasure hunting is a hobby of many people. It is called geocaching. People who do geocaching go treasure hunting. They call these treasures caches (**M1**, **M3**).
To find them, they can simply use their smartphone or any other GPS device.

M2 GPS satellite at work

GPS – A new technology

GPS is short for 'Global Positioning System'. More than 20 GPS satellites are 20,000 km above the surface of the Earth.
These satellites send signals to GPS devices – your smartphone, a GPS receiver or a car-navigation system, for example.

GPS devices can then calculate where you are on Earth. They show your position on the global grid (**M4**).

'Geocaching is just great! It is so much fun to look for caches. You can start pretty easily: just download a geo-caching app for your smartphone and this programme tells you where somebody hid a cache. It shows you the exact position as a combination of numbers and letters.
My dad says that every place on Earth has only one of these combinations and that they tell us the position on the global grid. Car-navigation systems can do that, too. But I'm not sure what the global grid is ...'

M3 Alex and his friends finding a cache

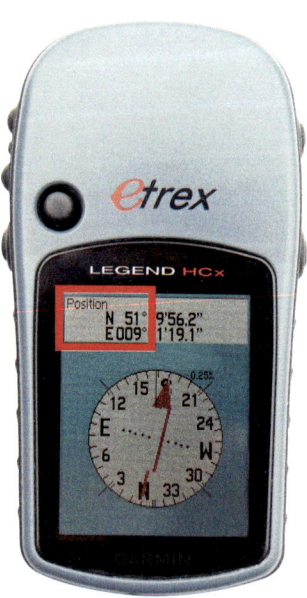

M4 Display of a GPS receiver

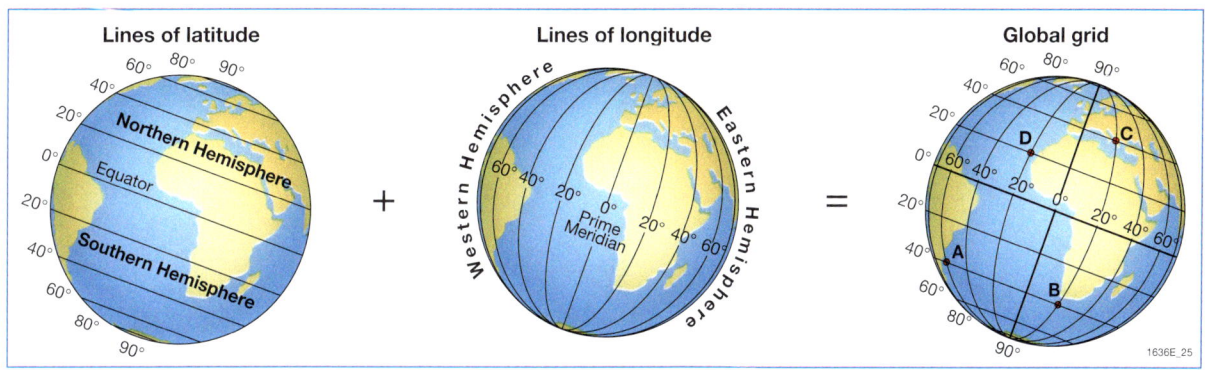

M5 The global grid

The location of places on Earth

We can locate every single place on Earth with the help of only two lines (M5):

▬ Lines of latitude run round the Earth from east to west. The Equator is at 0 degrees. It divides the Earth into the Northern Hemisphere and the Southern Hemisphere. The Equator is the longest line of latitude (40,075 km).

The North Pole is at 90 degrees north (90° N), the South Pole is at 90 degrees south (90° S). They are the shortest lines of latitude – in fact, they are only dots.

We number lines of latitude from 0° to 90°. We label them with the letter N for the lines in the Northern Hemisphere and with S for the lines in the Southern Hemisphere.

||| Lines of longitude run from the North Pole to the South Pole and back to the North Pole. Half of this line is a meridian. The Prime Meridian is at 0° and runs through Greenwich (London).

The Prime Meridian divides the Earth into the Western Hemisphere and the Eastern Hemisphere. We label them with the letter W for the lines in the Western Hemisphere and with E for the lines in the Eastern Hemisphere.

Together, these two sets of lines form a grid. We call it the global grid (M5, M6). The exact location of a place is where lines of longitude and latitude meet.

M6 'The Earth in a net'

HELPFUL WORDS AND PHRASES
for TASK 2:
- (Place) ... lies at ...
- (Place) ... is at ...
- (Place) ... is located ...
- (Place) ... is situated ...
- The exact location of ... is ... on the global grid.

> **HOW TO SAY ...where a place is on the global grid**
>
> Example: Where is place 'D' in M5?
> Say: 'Place 'D' is at twenty degrees north and twenty degrees west.'
> Write: 'Place 'D' is at 20° N / 20° W.'

TASKS

1. Describe the global grid in German.
2. Locate places A, B and C in M5.
3. Locate your home on the global grid.
4. For experts: Show the connection between geocaching and the global grid.

KEY TERMS

- Equator
- global grid
- Global Positoning System (GPS)
- line of longitude
- line of latitude
- meridian
- Northern Hemisphere
- Prime Meridian
- Southern Hemisphere
- surface

Time Zones

At the same moment, some parts of the Earth are in light and other parts are in darkness (› pp. 14-15). It can be early in the morning in some places and evening in others. For this reason there are time zones (**M1**, **M2**).

The time zones run nearly parallel to the lines of longitude (› p. 17). For every 15 degrees of longitude there is an hour time difference.
Normally places that are directly north or south of each other have the same time. The International Date Line follows the 180° meridian. When you cross it, the date changes.

M1 The World Time Clock in Berlin, Germany

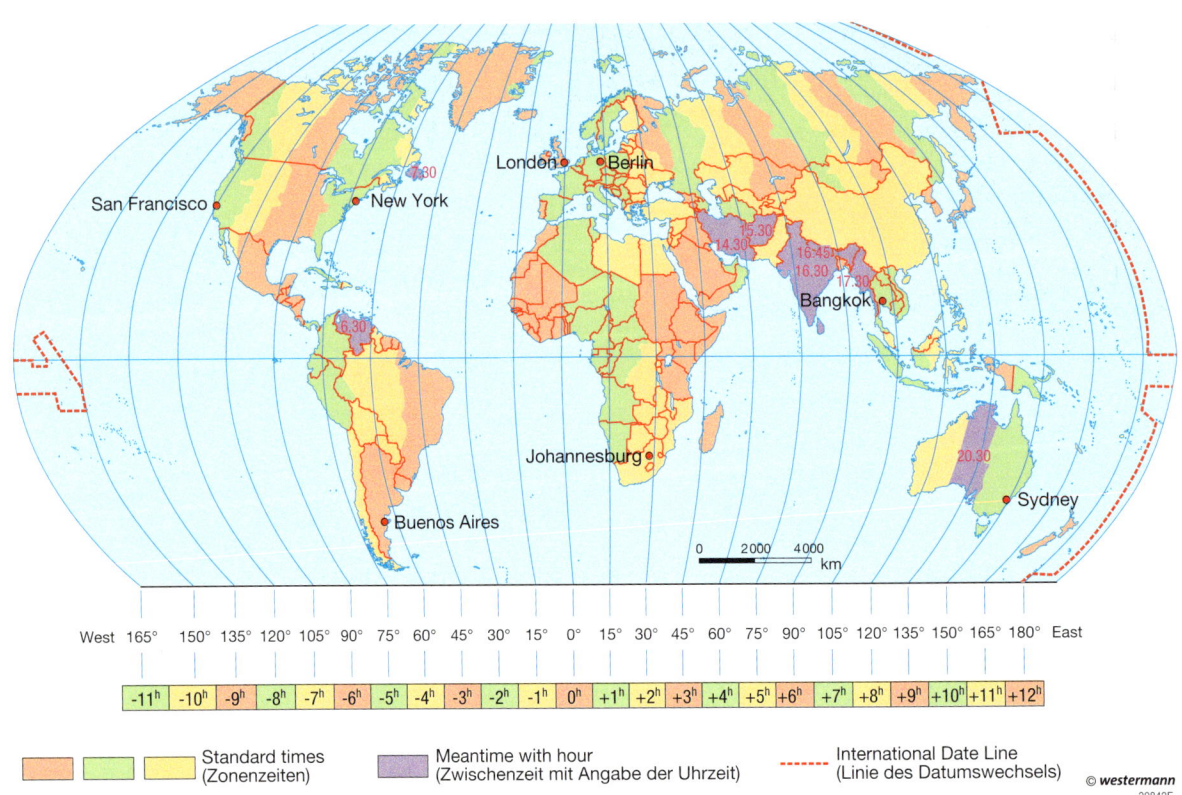

M2 The time zones

Sandrito (Peru) Lisanne (Netherlands) Kimiko (Japan)

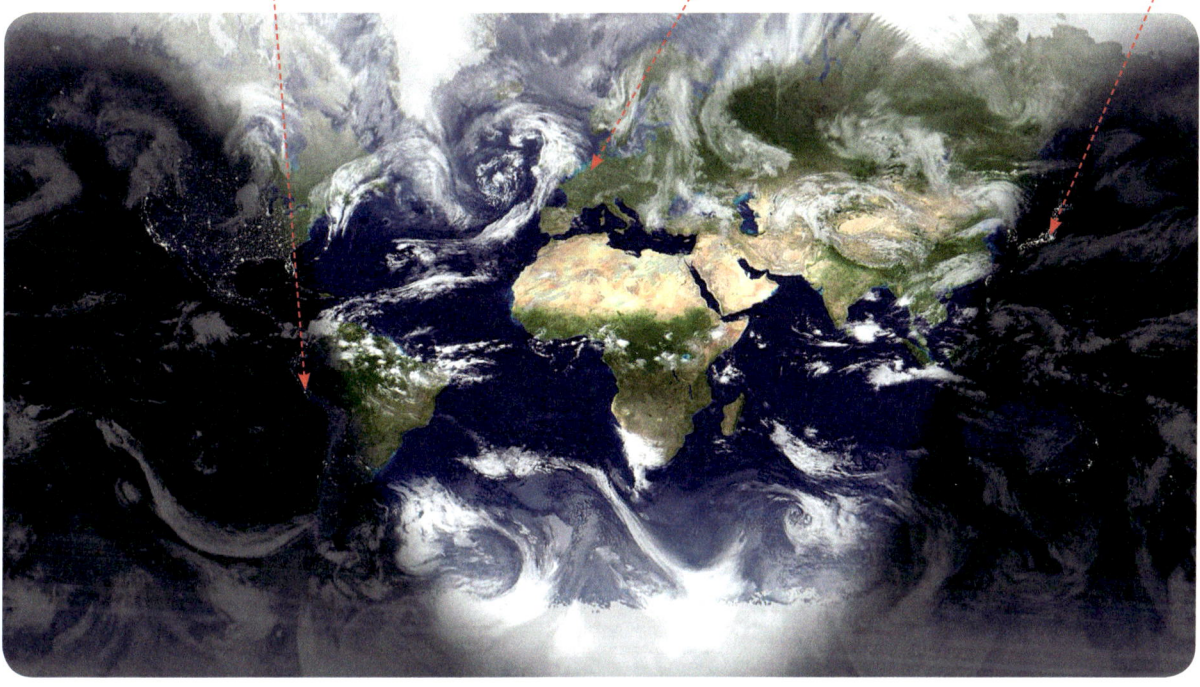

M3 A video conference

TASKS

1. Name five countries from another continent that are in the same time zone as Germany. Use **M2**.
2. It is 6 p.m. in Amsterdam. Lisanne wants to start a video conference with Kimiko. Explain what time is ideal to talk.
3. Sandrito wants to talk to Lisanne and Kimiko. Explain what time is ideal for all three people.

KEY TERMS

- International Date Line
- time difference
- time zone

HELPFUL WORDS AND PHRASES

for TASK 1:
- … are located on the same line of longitude as Germany.
- When it is … o'clock in Germany, it is … in …

for Task 3:
- … o'clock is perfect for all three people, because…
- In Peru/ the Netherlands/Japan it is …. o'clock, so…

19

M1 The seasons

Reasons for Seasons

Tilted axis

The Earth orbits the Sun once a year. The Earth's axis is tilted at an angle of 23.5° (M3). This tilt stays the same while the Earth orbits the Sun. Because of the tilted axis different parts of the Earth face the Sun in the course of the travel:
The North Pole faces the Sun between March and September. The South Pole faces the Sun between September and March (M2).

Vertical and oblique rays

The Sun's rays light and heat the Earth. Some places get more light and heat than other places: Vertical rays heat up the Earth's surface more than oblique rays, because they concentrate on a smaller area (M4).
Because of the tilted axis, more vertical rays reach the Northern Hemisphere between June and September. Then it is warm there and we call this summer.

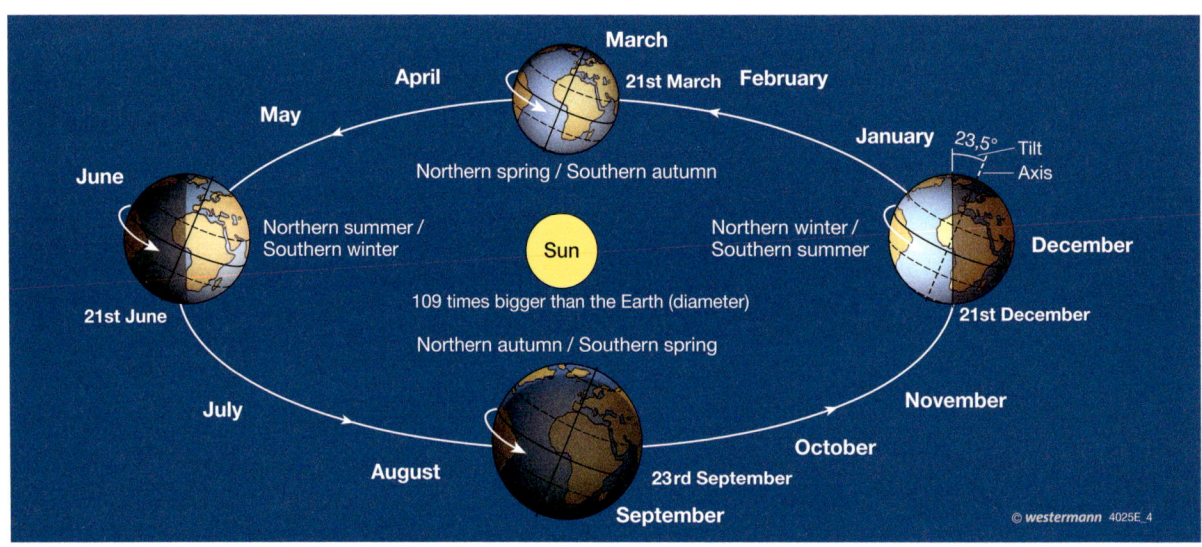

M2 The way of the Earth around the Sun

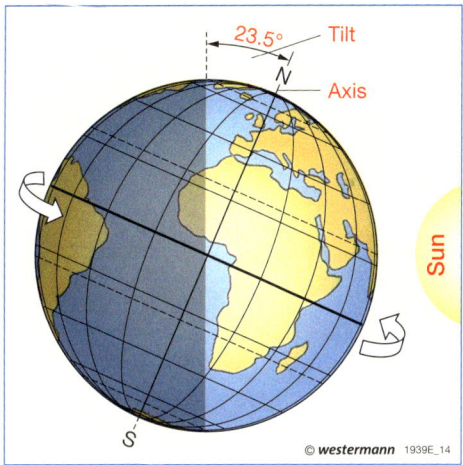

M3 The tilted axis

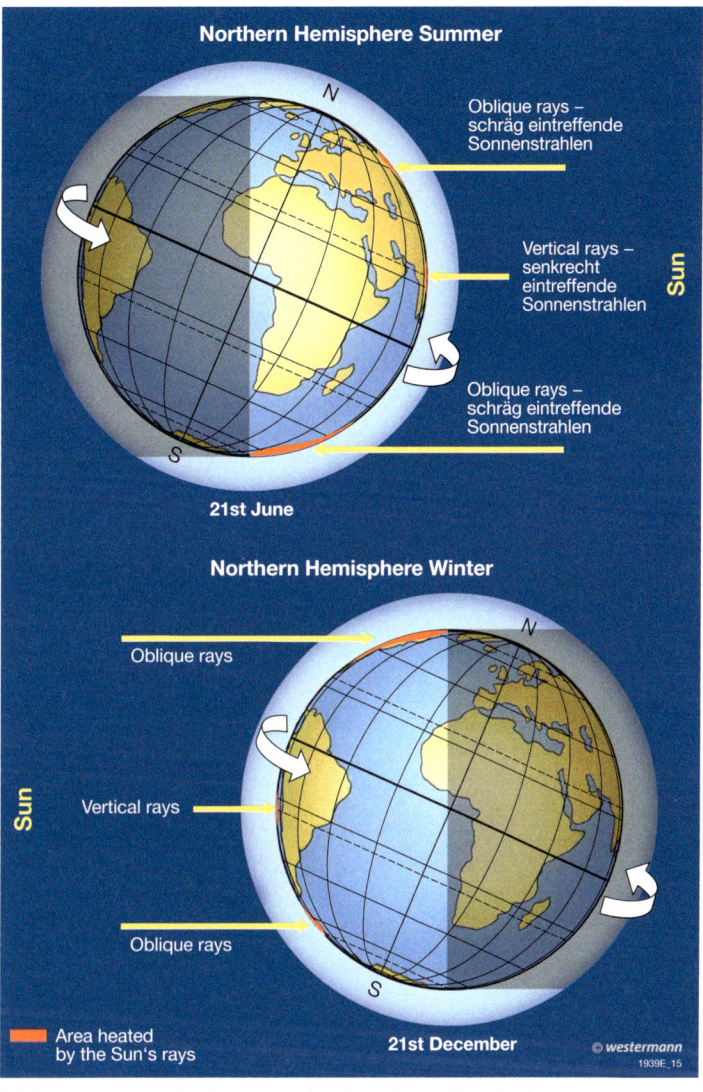

M4 Summer and winter in the Northern Hemisphere

Between December and March, fewer vertical rays reach the Northern Hemisphere. Then it is cold there and we call this winter. On the southern half of the Earth, summer is between December and March and winter is between June and September.
The Poles get so little light and heat from the Sun that ice covers them the whole year. The Equator gets so much light and heat from the Sun that it is hot the whole year (M4).

TASKS

1. a) Match the seasons with the correct picture in **M1**.
   b) Describe differences you can see in these pictures.
2. Set up an experiment to show how the Sun's rays light the Earth in June and December (**M2**).
   Use a round object (apple, ball, ...) and a flashlight.
3. Explain in English and in German why we have the seasons.

KEY TERMS

- Earth's axis
- Northern Hemisphere
- oblique rays
- season
- Southern Hemisphere
- tilt
- vertical rays

HELPFUL WORDS AND PHRASES
for TASK 3:

- The Earth orbits ..., so ...
- Different parts of the Earth face the Sun ...
- Because of ... more oblique rays reach the ... Hemisphere.
- When it is winter in Europe, the Northern Hemisphere gets ...
- But in summer ...
- In the Southern Hemisphere, the seasons are ...
- The North and South Pole only ...
- Around the Equator there are always ...

What is Weather?

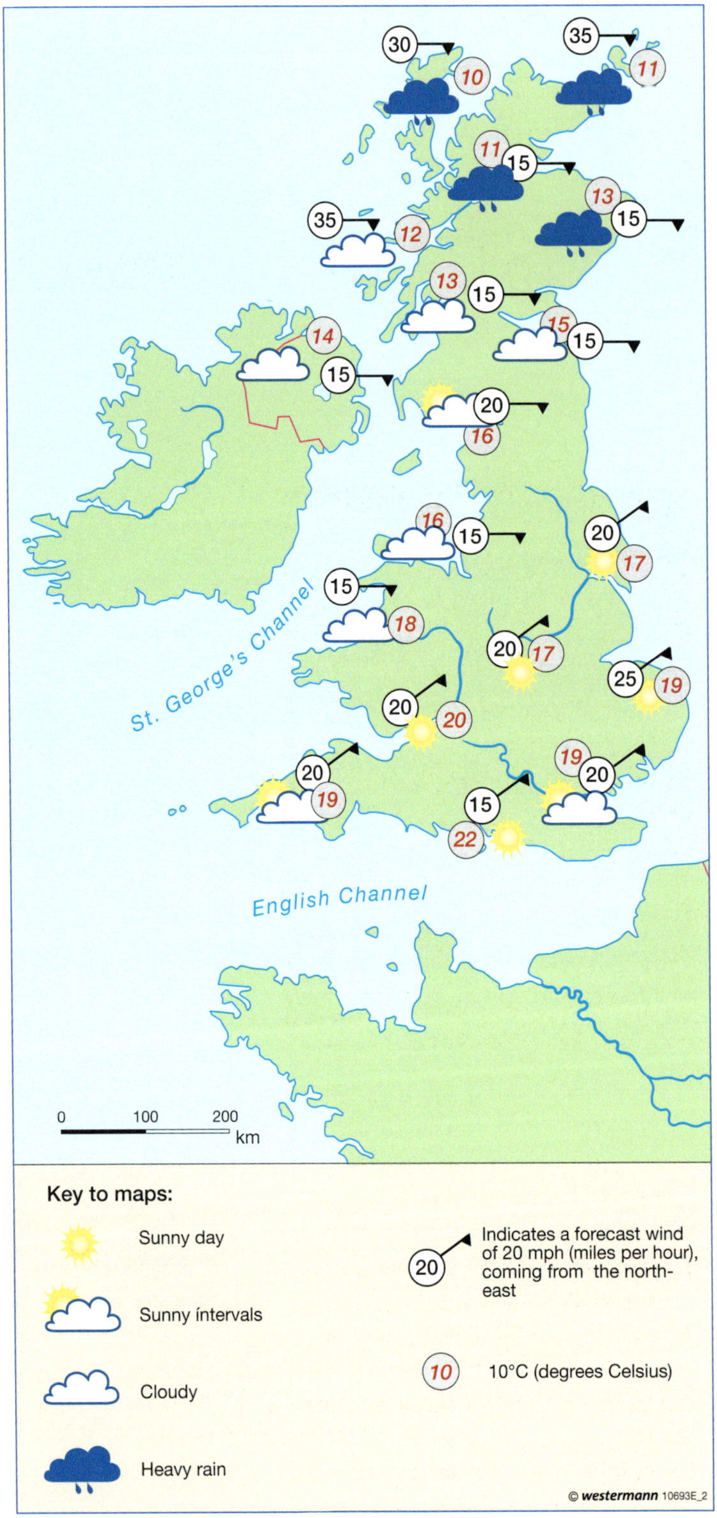
St. George's Channel
English Channel
0 100 200 km
Key to maps:
Sunny day
Sunny intervals
Cloudy
Heavy rain
Indicates a forecast wind of 20 mph (miles per hour), coming from the north-east
10°C (degrees Celsius)
© westermann 10693E_2

M1 Weather situation in the UK on a day in September

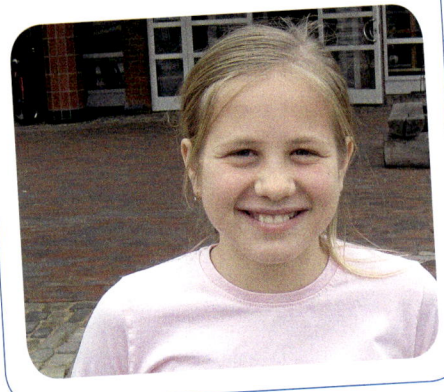

'Hi, I'm Amy.
I live in Aberdeen. That's in the north of Scotland. I think I have to take the bus to the city today, because it's rainy and windy here outside. It's only 13 degrees Celsius and there are heavy rain showers. I need my pullover and an umbrella today.'

M2 Amy from Aberdeen

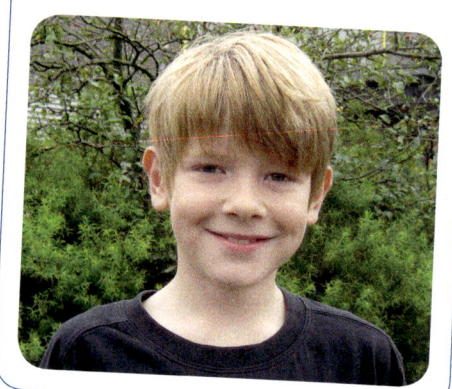

'Hi, I'm Matthew.
I live in Eastbourne. That's in the south of England. I will go swimming with some of my friends this afternoon, because it's very sunny and warm outside. It's about 22 degrees Celsius and there are no clouds. So I can wear my new shorts today, too!'

M3 Matthew from Eastbourne

M4 In Aberdeen (› Amy)

M6 In Eastbourne (› Matthew)

The weather forecast

'Today is Saturday. It's very cloudy in Aberdeen with only 13 degrees Celsius. Tomorrow it will be rainy with 14 degrees Celsius, but on Tuesday and Wednesday it will be sunny. The temperature will be 12 degrees Celsius on Tuesday and 13 degrees Celsius on Wednesday. That's pretty cold, but my friends and I can still go to the park before there will be rain showers on Thursday again. I hope the weather will be nice at the next weekend!'

Aberdeen Hourly		13°
SUNDAY	🌧	14° 4°
MONDAY	☀	13° 7°
TUESDAY	☀	12° 8°
WEDNESDAY	☀	13° 7°
THURSDAY	🌧	13° 6°
FRIDAY	☀	14° 9°

Updated 15/09/2013 12:12

HELPFUL WORDS AND PHRASES
for TASK 1, 2:

- The weather is (partly) sunny / cloudy …
- The temperature is about … degrees Celsius.
- There are some / heavy rain showers in …
- It is (not) windy.
- The wind speed is … mph.
- In the north / north-east …

M5 Amy uses a smartphone-app and makes a weather forecast for Aberdeen

The weather elements
To describe the weather you look at different weather elements, e.g.: wind, precipitation (rain, snow, fog, hail, showers, drizzle), temperature, clouds, and air pressure. Together, the weather elements make the weather situation of a place. The weather situation can change several times a day. You can use a weather map to describe and forecast the weather.

TASKS
1. Describe the weather in different parts of Great Britain (M1).
2. Tell Amy and Matthew what the weather is like at your place.
3. Watch a weather report on the news. Write a text in English or in German: What will the weather be like in your area tomorrow? Only talk about precipitation, temperature and wind.

KEY TERMS
- forecast
- precipitation
- temperature
- weather
- weather elements

M1 Professional rain gauge

M3 Self-made rain gauge

How Can We Measure and Record …

…temperature?

A minimum and maximum thermometer (M2) measures the highest and lowest temperature over a period of time in degrees Celsius (°C).
The thermometer must be in the shade.
It stands about 2 metres (m) off the ground.

…precipitation?

You can measure precipitation with the help of a rain gauge (M1, M3).
This instrument measures the amount of precipitation over a certain period of time in millimetres (mm).

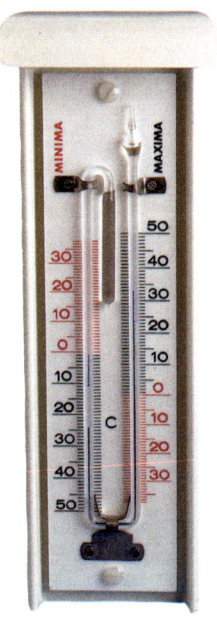

M2 Minimum and maximum thermometer

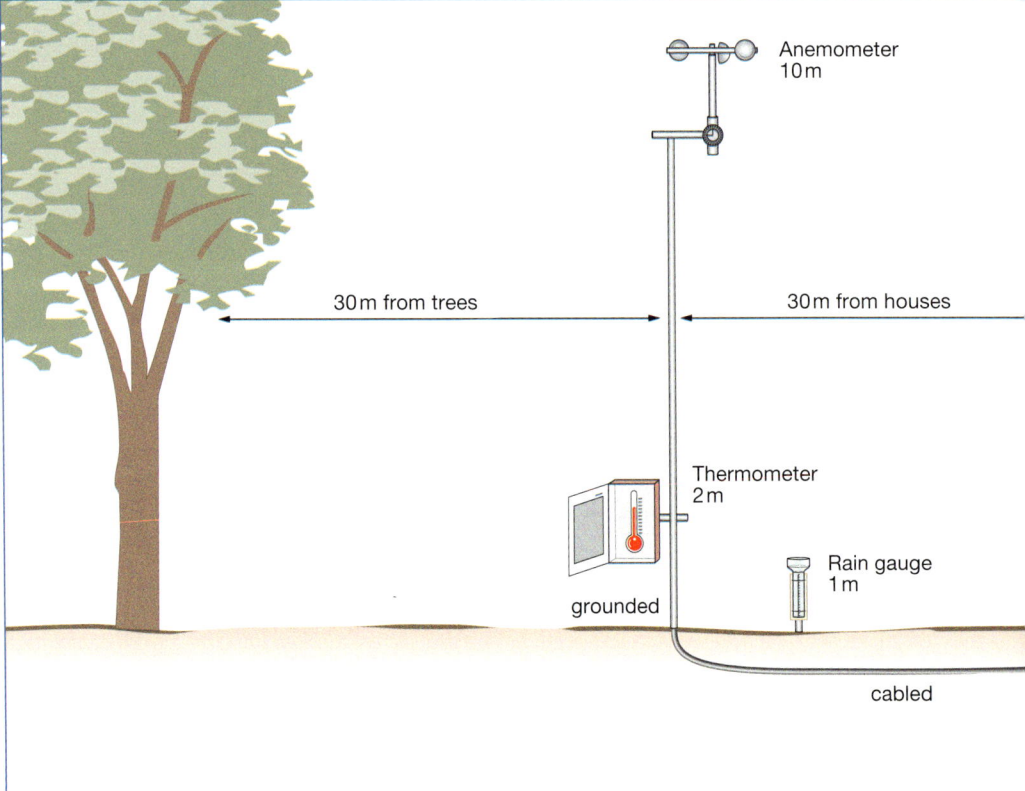

M4 A weather station measures and records the weather for a certain location

M5 Windsock showing the wind direction

M6 Cup anemometer for schools showing the wind speed

...wind?

A windsock shows the wind direction and the wind speed (**M5**).

The cup anemometer (**M6**) measures the wind speed. The cups of the anemometer spin round. The number of revolutions in a given time gives the wind speed in miles per hour (mph).

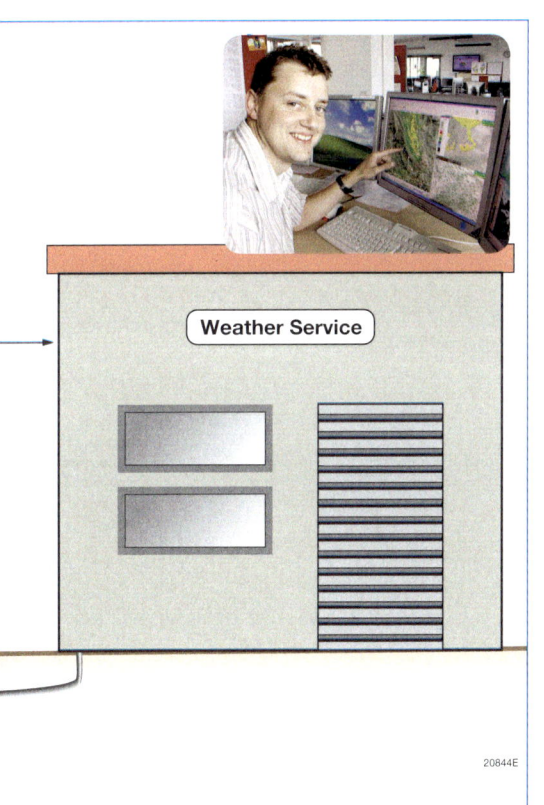

M7 Digital weather station for private use

TASKS

1 a) Measure the temperature at the same time of the day for one week.
b) Draw a table and describe what you find out.

2 a) Make your own rain gauge with the help of **M3**.
b) Measure and record the precipitation for one week. (Do not forget to empty your rain gauge every day.)
c) Describe what you have found out.

HELPFUL WORDS AND PHRASES
for TASK 1, 2:

- On Monday ... the temperature /precipitation was ... °C/mm.
- The highest / lowest ... was ...
- The minimum / maximum ... was ...
- The temperature ... was between ... and ...

KEY TERMS

- anemometer
- rain gauge
- thermometer
- weather station
- windsock
- wind speed

Different Landscapes

As temperature, precipitation and relief can be very different from place to place, you can find different landscapes on Earth, too. Some of them are extreme because extreme forms of climate influence them (**M1**, **M2**, **M3**).

In tropical rainforests near the Equator it is warm and it rains a lot throughout the year. The weather there is similar every day with high temperatures and heavy rainfall in the afternoons. There is very dense forest vegetation with many different animals. In this climate, you can grow crops throughout the year.

M1 Tropical rainforest

In deserts it is often very hot during the day with only very little precipitation. Sometimes it does not rain for years. There can be huge differences in the temperatures: while there is extreme heat in the daytime, it can get very cold at night. The vegetation is mostly rather sparse.
In many parts of deserts there is no vegetation at all. Sand or stones cover large areas. Except from oases, it is too dry to grow crops in deserts.

M2 Desert

Climate
The climate describes the average weather conditions of a certain region over a period of at least 30 years.

In the polar regions near the North Pole and the South Pole it is extremely cold. Most of the time, temperatures are far below zero and if there is precipitation, it usually falls as snow. So near the Poles there is no vegetation. And of course, as the temperatures are so low you cannot grow crops there.

M3 Polar region

TASKS

1. Describe the photos in **M1**, **M2**, and **M3** in detail.
2. Draw a table of the climate, the vegetation, and the possibilities to grow crops in the tropical rainforest (**M1**), in the desert (**M2**), and in polar regions (**M3**).
3. Compare the regions with the help of your table (task 2).

KEY TERMS
- climate
- crop
- desert
- landscape
- polar region
- precipitation
- relief
- tropical rainforest
- vegetation

HELPFUL WORDS AND PHRASES
for TASK 3:
- The climate in ... is hotter / colder / dryer / wetter than in ...
- Compared to ..., ... are hotter / colder / dryer / wetter.
- The vegetation in ... is more / less dense than in ...

Germany and Europe

30 The Federal Republic of Germany
32 What Do Germany's Landscapes Look Like?
34 Discover Europe
36 Living Together in Europe
38 European Climatic Regions
40 Agriculture in Great Britain
42 An Arable Farm in Essex
44 Oil and Gas – Non-renewable Resources from the North Sea
46 Renewable Energy
48 Industries in the London Area
50 A European Aeroplane for the World
52 A Working Day in Edinburgh
54 Living in Edinburgh
56 The Many Sides of Tourism
58 Holidays in the Alps
60 Malta – A Famous Tourist Place

M1 Europe seen from space

1 2 3 4 5 6 7 8

The Federal Republic of Germany

M1 Physical map of Germany with state borders

9 10 11 12 13 14 15 16

Germany has got 16 states. Each state has got its own capital and its own parliament. As you can see on the map M1, some states are huge and others are very small.

The smallest state with the lowest number of inhabitants is Bremen. The largest state is Bavaria. The state North Rhine-Westphalia has got the highest number of big cities and inhabitants.

1 *Bremen*
2 *Bavaria*
3 *North Rhine-Westphalia*
4 *Baden-Württemberg*
5 *Rhineland-Palatinate*
6 *Saarland*
7 *Schleswig-Holstein*
8 *Lower Saxony*
9 *Hesse*
10 *Thuringia*
11 *Brandenburg*
12 *Saxony*
13 *Mecklenburg-Western Pomerania*
14 *Saxony-Anhalt*
15 *Hamburg*
16 *Berlin*

FACT SHEET

Country profile Germany

Population:	81,726,000
Capital:	Berlin (3.46 million)
Total area:	357,121 km²
Highest mountain:	Zugspitze (2,962 m)
Longest river:	Rhine (1,320 km)

Neighbouring countries:
Belgium, Denmark, France, Luxembourg, Netherlands, Austria, Poland, Switzerland, Czech Republic

M2 Some facts about Germany (2014)

FACT SHEET

State profile North Rhine-Westphalia

Population:	17,841,000
Capital:	Düsseldorf (0.59 million)
Total area:	34,092 km²
Highest mountain:	Langenberg (843m)
Longest river:	Lippe (255 km)

Neighbouring states:
Lower-Saxony, Hesse, Rhineland-Palatinate

M3 Some facts about North Rhine-Westphalia (2014)

www.statistik-portal.de

TASKS

1. List all the German states and their capitals in a table. Use your atlas.
2. Quiz: How well do you know Germany?
   a) Write down 6 statements about German states: 3 statements that are true and 3 statements that are false. Use **M1**.
   b) Ask your partner to find the mistakes. Here are two examples: The River Weser flows through Lower Saxony. Munich is located in Thuringia.
3. Choose one of Germany's states. Create a fact sheet of that state similar to **M3**. You can also add other interesting information (e.g. sights or lakes).

KEY TERMS

- capital
- inhabitant
- parliament
- population
- state

HELPFUL WORDS AND PHRASES

for TASK 2:
- ... (is) next to ...
- ... east / north / south-west ... of ...
- ... has got ...
- ... flows through ...
- ... is located ...

pp. 62-65 Atlas, Maps

D1-016
www.diercke.de

M1 Landscapes of Germany (A-D)

What Do Germany's Landscapes Look Like?

Germany has got four main types of landscape.
In the north there is the North German Plain with a relief that is mostly flat with only some hilly areas.
In the middle part you find the Central Uplands, a hilly and mountainous area with some mountains rising up to about 1,500 m. The Alpine Foreland and the Alps are in the south. The Alpine Foreland rises slowly from 300 m in the north to 800 m close to the Alps.
Finally, the Bavarian Alps have the relief of a steep mountain system with some places higher than 2,000 m.

M2 Map of German landscapes

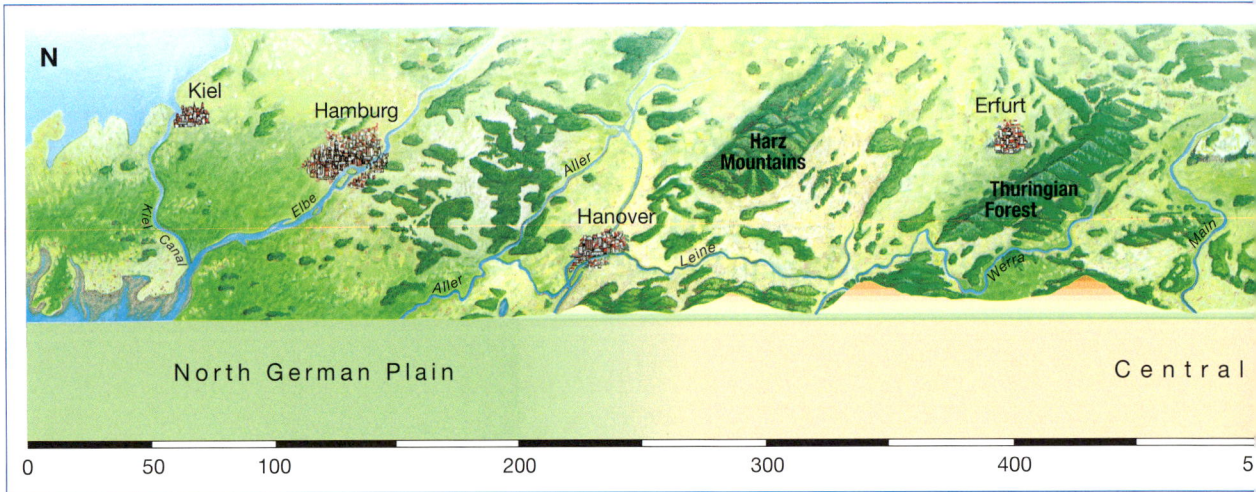

M3 From the coast to the Alps – cross section from M2

'Hi, I am Maria.
I like to spend my summer holidays at the sea! There are a lot of tourists. You can go swimming or play beach volleyball. My favourite island is Norderney. It is easy to make friends there. In winter, we often go the Alps for skiing!'

M4 Where Maria wants to spend her holidays in Germany

'Hi, I am Thomas.
I like action and that is why I spend all of my holidays in the Alps! In the summer we go climbing or I use my mountain bike. In the winter, I go snowboarding and I enjoy the views!'

M5 Where Thomas wants to spend his holidays in Germany

TASKS

1. Describe the photos A, B, C and D in **M1**.
2. Match the pictures and the German landscapes (**M2**).
3. Where do you want to spend your holidays in Germany? Give reasons.

KEY TERMS

- hilly area
- mountainous area
- plain
- relief
- upland

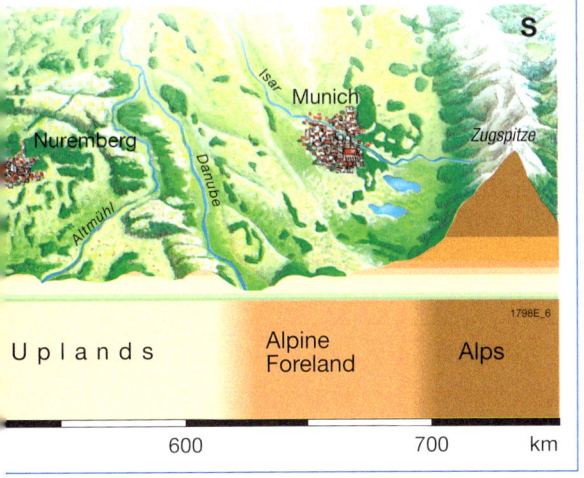

HELPFUL WORDS AND PHRASES

for TASK 1:
- ... in the north / middle part /... there is ...
- ... with a relief that is ... mostly flat / with only some hilly areas ...
- ... a hilly area ...
- ... a mountainous area ...
- ... some mountains rising up to about ... metres.
- ... a steep mountain system ...
- ... some places ... higher than ... metres.

Discover Europe

Europe is the second smallest of the seven continents. It has got over 40 countries with different languages, currencies and stamps. Europe's borders run through the Atlantic Ocean in the north and west. In the east it borders the Ural Mountains and the Mediterranean Sea in the south. Some countries have not got a coastline: they are landlocked. Twenty-eight of the European countries belong to the European Union (EU › p. 36-37). Two of the countries, Russia and Turkey, belong to Europe and Asia.

> **FACT SHEET**
>
> **Continent profile Europe**
>
> **Highest mountain:** Mont Blanc (4,807 m)
> **Biggest city:** Moscow (11,500,000)
> **Largest country:** Russia
> **Smallest country:** Vatican City
> **Longest river:** Volga (3,600 km)
> **Largest lake:** Lake Ladoga (17,700 km²)
> **Biggest island:** Great Britain
> (219,300 km²)

HELPFUL WORDS AND PHRASES
for TASK 3:
- I would like to tell you something about ...
- ... is in the north / south / east / southwest / ... of Europe.
- The capital of ... is ... .
- It is located in the north/ ...
- ... has got ... inhabitants.
- The highest mountain is ... . It is ... m high.
- The longest river is ...

M1 Some facts about Europe (2014)

Capital

Every country has got a capital city. In most countries there the government meets to make decisions. The capital is usually a centre of business and entertainment. This makes most capital cities the largest and most important city in the country.

M2 Political map of Europe

pp. 62-63 Atlas

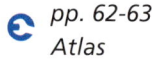

TASKS

1. Work in pairs: Partner A plans a trip from Lisbon to Kiev (west to east). Partner B plans a trip from Stockholm to Athens (north to south). Describe your routes to each other with the help of your atlas and **M2**. Which countries and cities do you pass?

❷ List all landlocked countries.
❸ For experts: Choose one European country. Prepare a short country profile about it (for example: location, people, language(s), rivers). Use the Internet for help and prepare a presentation in class.

KEY TERMS

- border
- capital
- landlocked country

35

M1 Open borders (example Frankfurt/Oder and Słubice)

M3 The Euro replaces national currencies

Living Together in Europe

Crossing borders has become easy

When people crossed borders in Europe in former times, they had to show their passports and go through customs. Sometimes this could take quite a long time.
The Netherlands, France, Belgium, Luxembourg and Germany were the first European countries where there were no checks at the border any longer.
Today this has become quite normal in many European countries and sometimes people do not even notice that they are passing a border (M1).

Shopping has become easy

People who travel to another country no longer have to exchange money. They can use the European currency, the Euro, in 18 member states (M2, M3). In addition it is easier to compare prices.

The European Union

In 1957 six countries formed the European Economic Community (EEC), which in 1967 became the European Community (EC). In 1993 the EC became the European Union (EU) with Brussels as its capital. Among others, the EU stands for freedom, peace and unity. The flag of the EU is a symbol of these principles (M6).

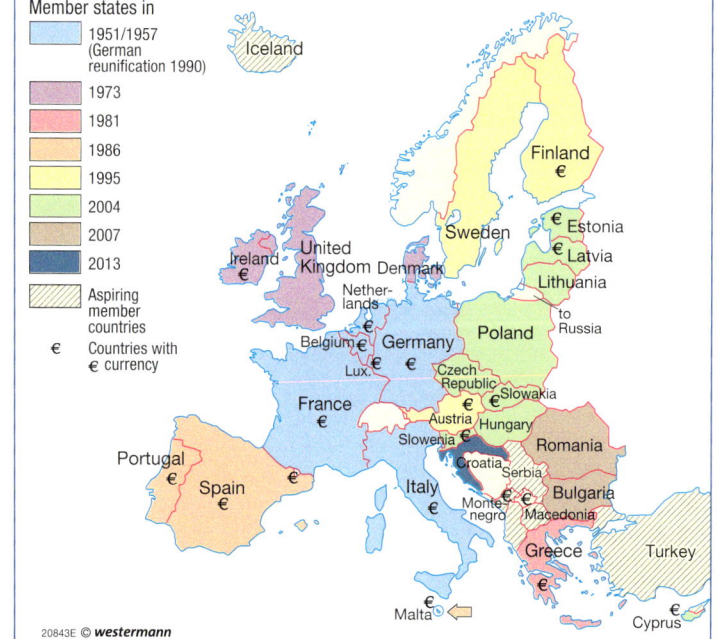

M2 Countries of the European Union (EU)

36

M4 Thalys at Cologne Central Station

M5 Aeroplanes connect Europe

Driving has become easy

The European Union has introduced common documents, such as ID-cards, passports, driving licences and number plates. Control is very easy because the police and other authorities in European member states understand the documents at once.

Travelling has become easy

High-speed trains link many big European cities. The Thalys, for example, runs from Cologne to Paris via Brussels (M4). Here people can change trains and travel to London using the Eurostar.

A motorway network links nearly all European countries, too. The E 45, for example, runs from Aarhus (Denmark) to Bologna (Italy) via Munich.

Airlines offer flights from even regional airports like Hahn/Frankfurt to destinations all over Europe, for example to Manchester or Reus/Barcelona.

Waterways, such as the Rhine-Main-Danube Canal, link the Europort of Rotterdam with central and southeastern Europe.

All these links together form a modern European transportation network.

M6 Flag of the European Union

www.europa.eu

TASKS

1. Describe the development of the EU since 1957 (M2 and Info 'The European Union').
2. Explain why living in Europe has become easier.
3. For experts: The four main institutions of the EU are:
   – the European Council,
   – the European Commission,
   – the European Parliament,
   – the European Court of Justice.
   Find out what they do and where they are located.

KEY TERMS

- customs
- Euro
- European transportation network
- European Union

HELPFUL WORDS AND PHRASES

for TASK 2:
- Today, there are no checks at the borders any longer, so …
- Because of the European currency …
- Because the EU has introduced common documents …
- European countries are linked by …, so …

M1 March in ...

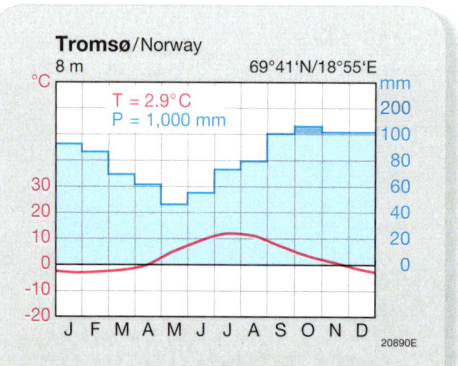

In the north-west of Europe there are some areas with long and cold winters and short and cool summers. The summers and winters are relatively wet and the precipitation in winter mostly falls as snow.

M3 Maritime climate in Norway

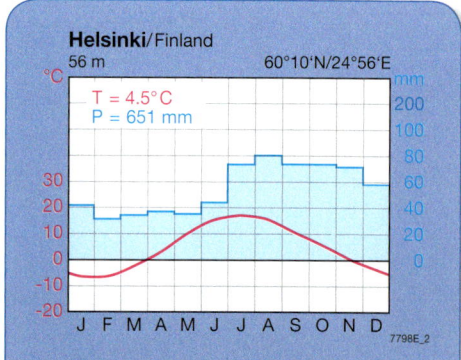

Finland is in the north-east of Europe. It has got cool and relatively dry summers and cold and dry winters. Most precipitation in winter falls as snow.

M5 Continental climate in Finland

European Climatic Regions

From Ireland in the west to Russia in the east, from Scandinavia in the north to the Mediterranean Sea in the south, the climate in Europe differs.

The climate changes from north to south and from west to east. Germany is located in the middle of Europe and has got a transitional type of climate.

M2 March in ...

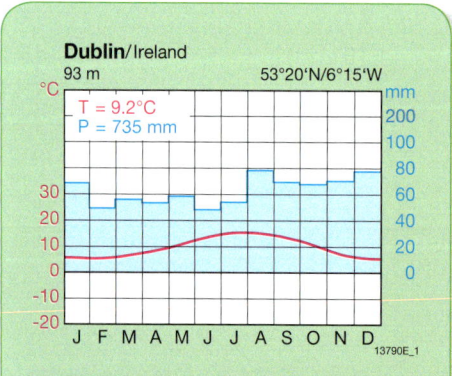

Ireland, the 'Green Island' has got mild winters and cool summers. So the temperature range is small. There is a constant amount of precipitation throughout the whole year. It is wet in summer and in winter.

M4 Maritime climate in Ireland

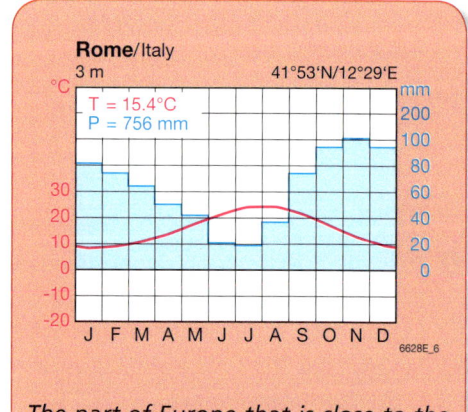

The part of Europe that is close to the Mediterranean Sea has got hot and dry summers and mild and wet winters.

M6 Mediterranean climate in Italy

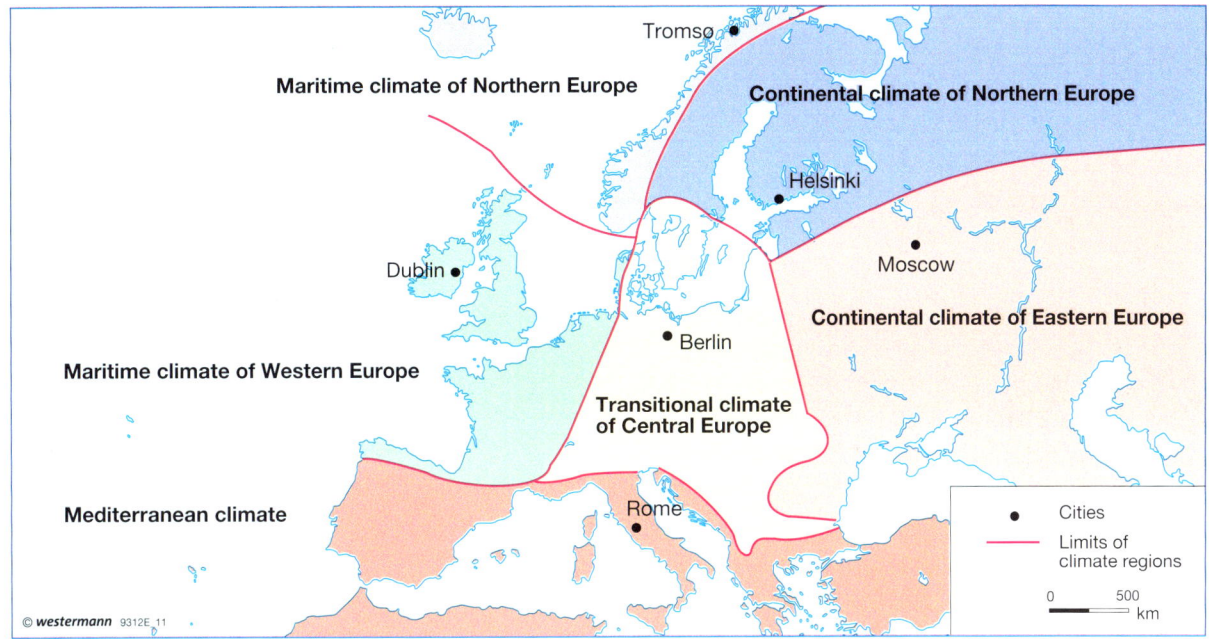

M7 Climatic regions of Europe

TASKS

1. Make a table. Note down in German the important characteristics of the different climatic regions of Europe.
2. Describe how the climate in Europe changes from north to south.
3. Describe how the climate in Europe changes from west to east.

KEY TERMS

- continental climate
- maritime climate
- Mediterranean climate
- temperature range
- transitional climate

HELPFUL WORDS AND PHRASES
for TASK 2:

- In the north / east ... the temperature is higher / lower than in the south / west ...
- There is less / more precipitation in ... than in ...
- Whereas the temperature / amount of precipitation in the ... is ... °C / mm it is ... °C / mm in the ...
- In contrast to ... there is less / more precipitation in ...
- In contrast to ... the temperature is higher / lower than in ...

Germany is located in central Europe. Germany has got warm and wet summers and cold and wet winters.

Russia has got hot summers and very cold winters. So the temperature range is high. The precipitation mostly falls in summer.

M8 Transitional climate in Germany

M9 Continental climate in Russia

pp. 66-67 Climate Graphs

39

Agriculture in Great Britain

Climate: Cool summers follow cold winters. Plenty of rainfall is good for the growth of grass.
Soils: The thin, poor soils are good enough for sheep grazing but not for other forms of farming.
Relief: The hilly, steep land is mostly not suitable for machines or cattle.
Products: The sheep give wool and meat.

M1 Hill farming

Climate: Warm summers and mild winters mean that cattle can be outside all year long. The high rainfall is good for the fast growth of grass.
Soils: They are fertile enough for grass growth, but not for arable farming.
Relief: We find only gentle slopes. Cattle cannot graze on land that is too steep.
Products: The cows produce milk, and, at the end of their lives, meat.

M2 Dairy farming

M3 Main farming types in Great Britain and Ireland

Soil

Most plants need soil to grow. They get their water, minerals and even air to breathe from the soil. The plants hold on to the soil with their roots.

Climate: Warm summers follow frosty winters. The yearly average temperature is 8 °C or more. There is little rainfall during the growing season.
Soils: The fertile soils are easy to plough.
Relief: It is mostly flat, so it is easy to use machines.
Products: The main crops are cereals, like wheat, and root crops, like potatoes.

M4 Arable farming

Climate: In huge greenhouses, farmers can control water and temperature. The outside climate is not so important.
Soils: Farmers improve the soil quality with fertilizers.
Relief: Greenhouses need flat land.
Products: They grow vegetables and flowers.

M5 Market gardening

TASKS

1 a) Make a table 'Farming Types of Great Britain'.
b) In your table, mark the farming type with A, B, C, or D which mainly depends on:
– moderate climate (A),
– fertile soil (B),
– flat relief (C),
– many workers (D).

2 Prepare and give a short talk about farming types in England in English or German.

KEY TERMS

- agriculture
- arable farming
- dairy farming
- farming type
- hill farming
- market gardening
- soil

HELPFUL WORDS AND PHRASES

Hints for TASK 1
Headings for columns:
- Farming types (M1, M2, M4, M5)

Headings for rows:
- Climate
- Soils
- Relief
- Products

41

 Peas
 Wheat
 Broad beans

M1 These are crops, farmer Fairs grows in contract farming

An Arable Farm in Essex

This is Mr. Fairs, a farmer in Essex. His farm is an arable farm.
When Lisa was on holiday in England, she interviewed him.

Lisa: Mr. Fairs, how big is your farm?
Mr. Fairs: That is difficult to say, because we farm not only our farm with 750 acres. We work for ten more farmers and do all the work on the fields for them: we plough, we sow, we harvest. This is 'contract farming'. Altogether we farm 4400 acres.
Lisa: That's a lot. In Germany only one in fifteen farms is bigger than 250 acres. You must have many workers!
Mr. Fairs: No, we don't. We use machines to do the work for us. My son and I have got only three permanent staff and three more staff at harvest time.

Lisa: What do you grow on your farm?
Mr. Fairs: We grow mostly wheat and we grow oilseed rape. We also grow peas and beans. All these crops will become animal feed.
Lisa: I like the yellow rape fields in the spring.
Mr. Fairs: More than a quarter of our fields are with rapeseed now. We get a good price for it at the moment. I guess it's because you can make so many things from it. You find all sorts of food in the supermarkets made with rapeseed oil. They even mix it into the petrol for the cars now. The government

M2 Rapeseed fields in May

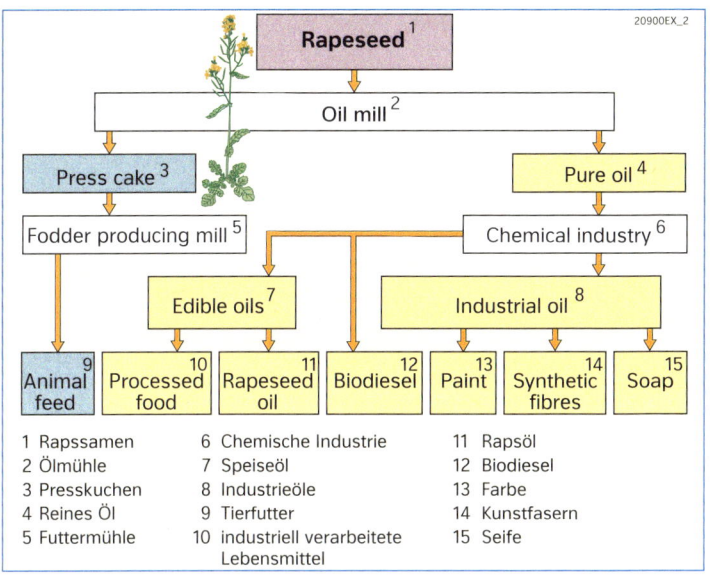

M3 Products from oilseed rape

Farmer Fairs harvests oilseed rape

In an oil mill

tells us to grow even more of it because it is a renewable resource. This means that you can harvest new oilseed rape every year.

Lisa: Are you a farmer or a businessman?

Mr. Fairs: Well. I'm both. This type of farming is agribusiness which means a business in agriculture. I spend most of the time in the office, my son looks after the machines and is out in the fields.

Lisa: I didn't see many machines around.

Mr. Fairs: Exactly! All our crops can be planted, grown and harvested with the same set of machines. For growing potatoes, for example, I would need different machines.

Lisa: Why are there no animals on your farm?

Mr. Fairs: Keeping animals would mean extra buildings, extra machines, and extra workers. And when you keep animals you have to be there every day of the week.

Today you have to specialize to earn money as a farmer. This part of Essex is best for arable farming. So you will see no cows or pigs around here.

Lisa: Thank you, Mr. Fairs!

A chemical plant

Rapeseed oil in the supermarket

M4 From field to kitchen

TASKS

1. Describe the way of rapeseed oil from the field to the kitchen (**M4**).
2. Draw farmer Fairs' business as a mind map. Compare your results.
3. Name the advantages of oilseed rape farming.

KEY TERMS

- agribusiness
- contract farming
- crop
- oilseed rape
- renewable resource

HELPFUL WORDS AND PHRASES

for TASK 1:
- The raw material is ...
- They separate the ... into ... and ...
- Then / After that ...
- In ... they turn ... into ...
- ... as well as ...
- The end products are ...

Oil and Gas – Non-renewable Resources from the North Sea

Today we use 87 million barrels of crude oil each day worldwide – that is a cube 240 m long, 240 m wide and 240 m high (M2). Refineries separate the oil into different products. 85 per cent of these products become energy. We burn oil products to drive our vehicles, to produce electricity and for heating and cooking. But crude oil, like natural gas, is a non-renewable resource. Once we burn it, it is gone.

In search of energy, the big oil companies found oil and gas fields under the North Sea. Drilling and extracting oil and gas from there is not easy. Sometimes more than 300 km away from the nearest coast, offshore drilling platforms are above the oil fields (M1). From there, the companies often use pipelines to transport the raw materials to a harbour with an oil or a gas terminal. Tankers, too, transport the oil and gas to these terminals. Then the crude oil flows through pipelines to the nearest refinery (M3).

Getting oil and gas from the North Sea is very costly. It can be highly dangerous and oil is poisonous. Oil spills from platforms, tankers or pipelines can kill marine life and put tourists off. Moreover, oil can burn and there are always risks of fires (M4).

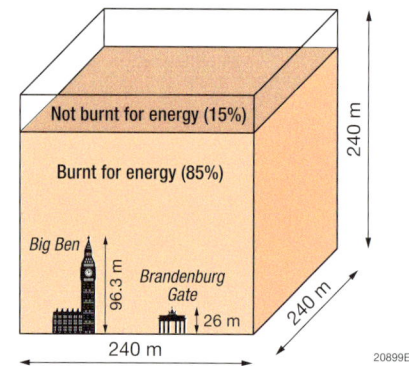

M2 Crude oil use per day worldwide

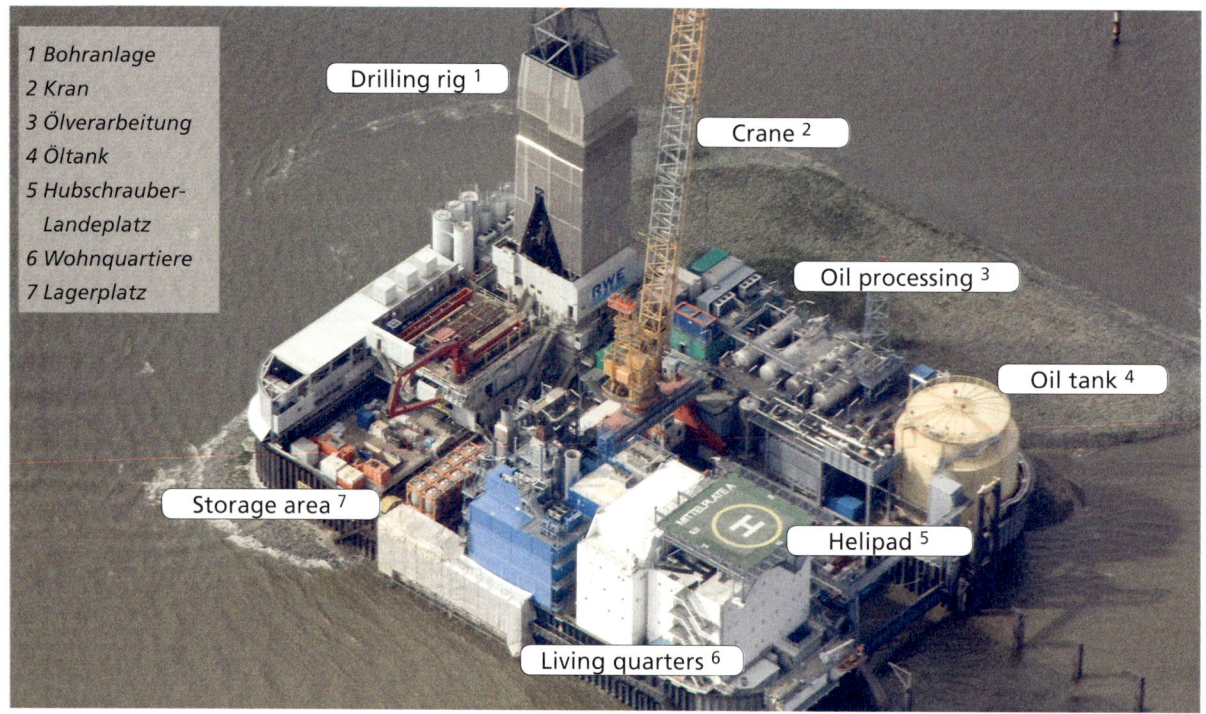

1 Bohranlage
2 Kran
3 Ölverarbeitung
4 Öltank
5 Hubschrauber-Landeplatz
6 Wohnquartiere
7 Lagerplatz

M1 Offshore oil platform 'Mittelplate' in the North Sea

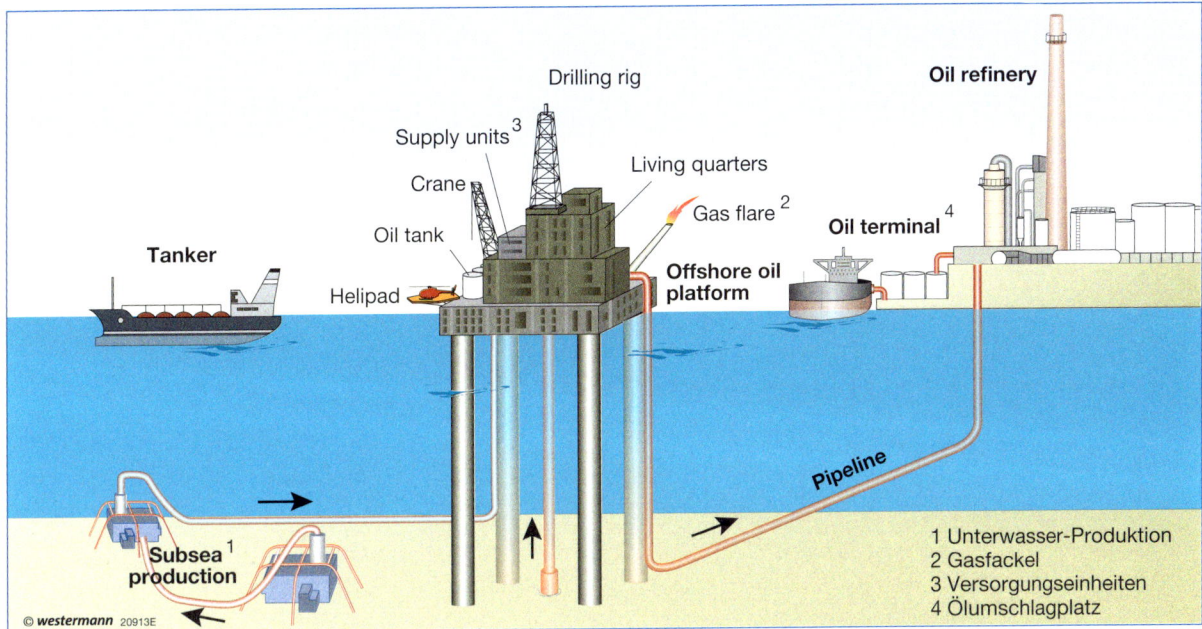

M3 From the oil field to the refinery

Crude oil and water pollution
1 litre of oil can cause the pollution of 1,000,000 litres of water.

Non-renewable energy
Non-renewable energy sources are raw materials which we burn to produce electricity or other forms of energy. Most of the non-renewable energies are fossil fuels like lignite, coal, crude oil and natural gas. Furthermore there is uranium which is used as fuel in nuclear power stations. We use up the non-renewable energies, so they are getting less and less.

M4 Burning offshore oil platform

TASKS

1. Use the text and the pictures to show the way of oil and gas from the oil field to the petrol station in a flow chart.
2. Inform yourself about an oil spill and report about it in class (in English or German).

KEY TERMS

- crude oil
- gas terminal
- natural gas
- non-renewable resource
- offshore oil platform
- oil field
- oil terminal
- oil spill
- pipeline
- raw material
- refinery

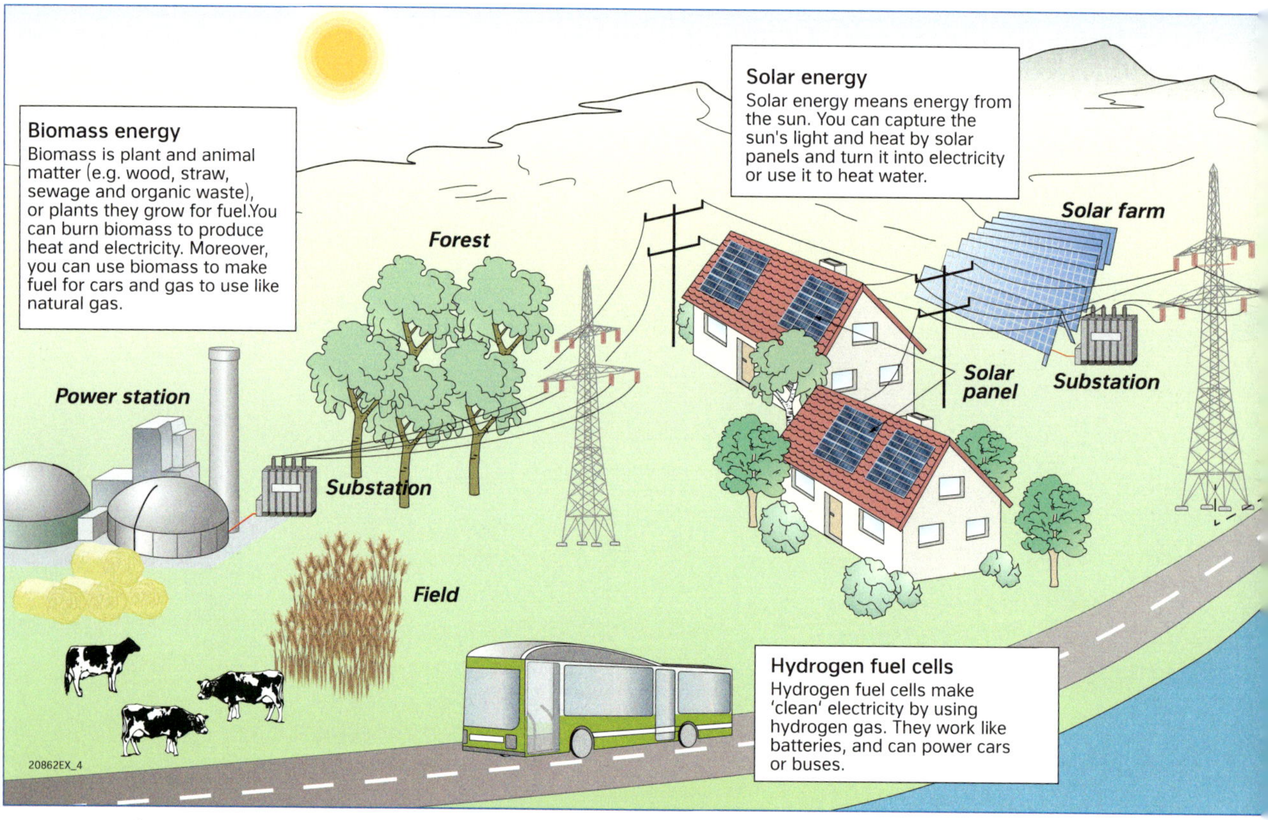

Biomass energy
Biomass is plant and animal matter (e.g. wood, straw, sewage and organic waste), or plants they grow for fuel. You can burn biomass to produce heat and electricity. Moreover, you can use biomass to make fuel for cars and gas to use like natural gas.

Solar energy
Solar energy means energy from the sun. You can capture the sun's light and heat by solar panels and turn it into electricity or use it to heat water.

Hydrogen fuel cells
Hydrogen fuel cells make 'clean' electricity by using hydrogen gas. They work like batteries, and can power cars or buses.

M1 Forms of renewable energy

Renewable Energy

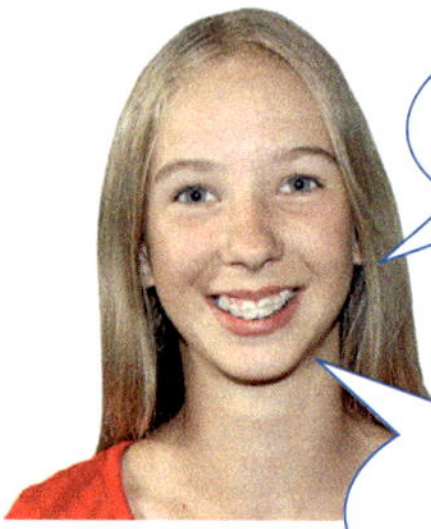

What is renewable energy?

Renewable energy comes from sources that will not run out, including the wind, the sun, the waves and tides, natural underground heat, energy crops, wood and waste. We can use renewable energy to produce electricity and heat for homes, businesses and transport.

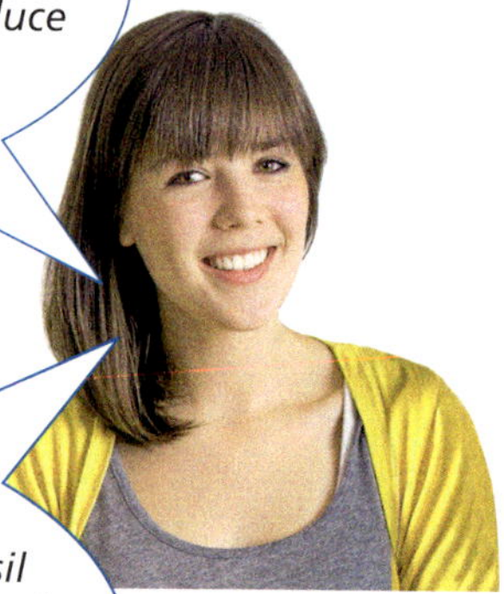

Why do we need renewable energy?

Most of the energy we use comes from non-renewable sources, such as oil and gas. These 'fossil fuels' are running out. Burning them to make energy also produces gases that play a part in climate change.
Renewable sources of energy do not run out or pollute the environment.

46

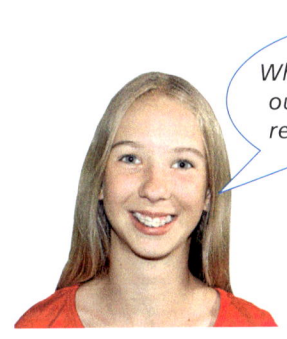

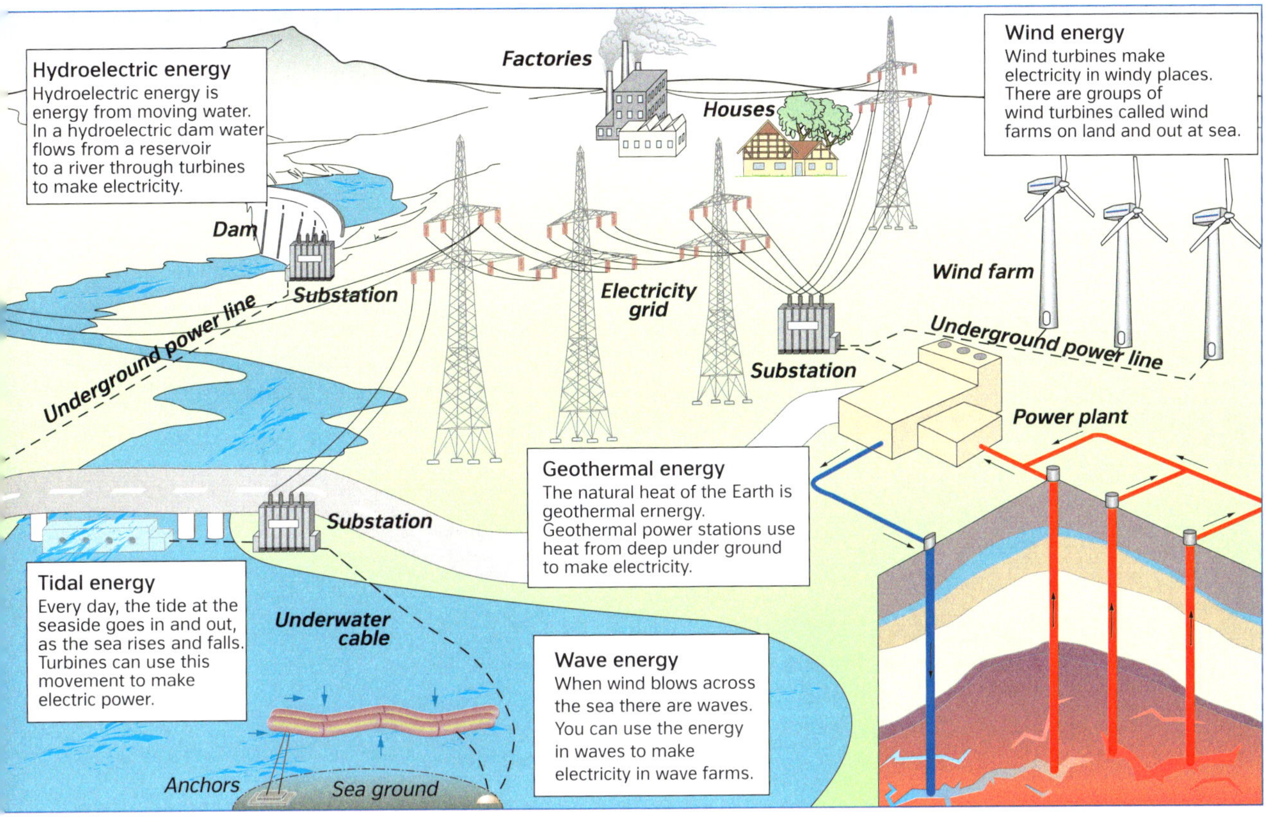
Hydroelectric energy
Hydroelectric energy is energy from moving water. In a hydroelectric dam water flows from a reservoir to a river through turbines to make electricity.
Factories
Houses
Wind energy
Wind turbines make electricity in windy places. There are groups of wind turbines called wind farms on land and out at sea.
Dam
Substation
Underground power line
Electricity grid
Wind farm
Underground power line
Substation
Power plant
Geothermal energy
The natural heat of the Earth is geothermal ernergy. Geothermal power stations use heat from deep under ground to make electricity.
Substation
Tidal energy
Every day, the tide at the seaside goes in and out, as the sea rises and falls. Turbines can use this movement to make electric power.
Underwater cable
Wave energy
When wind blows across the sea there are waves. You can use the energy in waves to make electricity in wave farms.
Anchors
Sea ground

Why don't we get all our electricity from renewable energy?

It is important to have a mix of energy sources so, if one fails, we can use another one. Moreover, many renewable technologies are still new and we do not know yet how to use them properly.

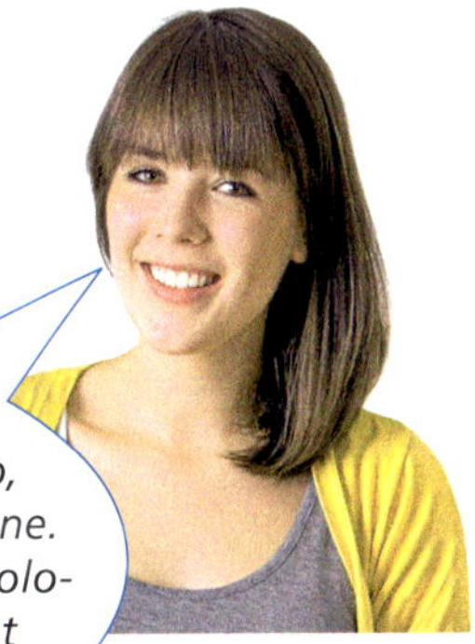

TASKS

1. Make a table of the renewable energies and their sources.
2. In a group of three, prepare a talk about one of the renewable energies and present it to the class.
3. Compare renewable and non-renewable energies in a short text.

KEY TERMS

- biomass energy
- geothermal energy
- hydroelectric energy
- hydrogen fuel cells
- power station
- renewable energy
- solar energy
- tidal energy
- wave energy
- wind energy

HELPFUL WORDS AND PHRASES

for TASK 3:

- ... are similar because ...
- ... differ because ...
- In contrast, ...
- Moreover, ...
- On the one hand ... on the other hand ...

M1 The machine construction industry makes machines and its parts

M3 The financial industry includes banks, insurances and similar industries

Industries in the London Area

London is one of the largest cities in Europe and one of the most important business centres in the world. The people who live in London need places to work and places where they can buy all the things and get all the services they need for their lives. You can see the most important London industries on the photos.

Industries

There are three main types of industries in three sectors. All industries in the primary sector deal with raw materials: farming, forestry, fishing and mining. Industries in the secondary sector are called the manufacturing industries which make, build, and put together finished products.

The tertiary sector is the service sector. People working in the service industries produce services instead of end products.

Sometimes a quaternary sector splits off from the tertiary sector. The quaternary industries include all the services dealing with information.

 pp. 64-65 Maps

M2 The food industry produces nearly everything we eat and drink

M4 The optical industry makes screens, lasers and other optical instruments

M5 The chemical industry produces e.g. plastic, paint, fertilizer, and medicine

M7 A refinery is at the end of pipelines or in harbours. It uses crude oil to produce petrol, heating oil and raw materials for the chemical industry

TASKS

1. Find examples of how you or your family use products and services from the industries you see in the photos.
2. In class, set up a 'jigsaw' to compare the industries around London, Paris and Berlin. Prepare a talk on your topic.
3. Translate the info box into German.

KEY TERMS

- manufacturing industry
- primary sector
- raw material
- secondary sector
- service industry
- tertiary sector
- quaternary industry

M8 The logistics industry stores goods in warehouses and transports them

M6 The electronics industry produces high-tech goods like computers, mobile telephones, and TV sets

M9 The media industry produces newspapers, radio, and TV programmes

M1 Parts of an aeroplane (Airbus A380)

A European Aeroplane for the World

Flying by aeroplane is safe and quick. Today more people use aeroplanes than ever before. They fly on business trips or go on holiday. So the airlines need more aeroplanes.

The world's biggest maker of aeroplanes is a European company, Airbus S.A.S. It has got 19 plants in four different countries in Western Europe (M2).

More than 60,000 people work for Airbus in Great Britain, France, Spain and Germany (M7) and more than 100,000 in supply companies in Western Europe, the United States and China. Supply companies produce parts for the aeroplanes. Rolls-Royce in England, for example, makes the engines. The supply companies then send the parts to one of the Airbus plants. Here they use all the components to make parts for the aeroplane, for example the cockpit.

All aeroplane parts come together in Toulouse in southern France for the final assembly. From there they fly to Hamburg for furnishing and painting.

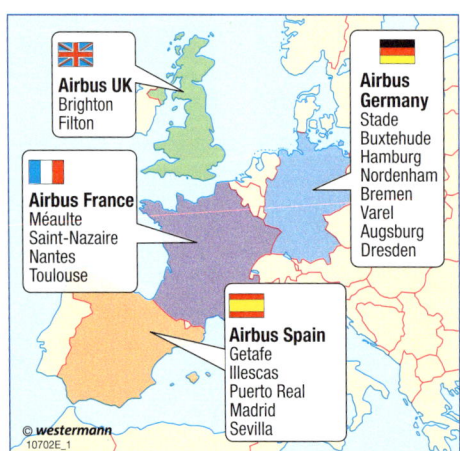

M2 Airbus manufacturing sites in Europe (2013)

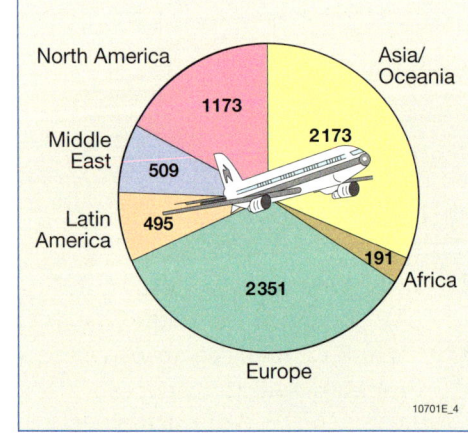

M3 Number of Airbuses all over the world (2013)

M4 Loading a barge on the Weser River

M5 Transport by aeroplane in Hamburg

M6 Vessel in the Atlantic Ocean

M8 Truck transport in southern France

The Airbus A380

One of the latest products in the Airbus family is the Airbus A380, which is one of the biggest passenger aeroplanes in the world. It can carry up to 800 passengers.
In the photos you can see the different ways to transport aeroplane parts to the final assembly plant in Toulouse. To be able to transport these parts, they had to build new roads, because some of the old ones were not wide enough. They built new ports because the old ports were not deep enough. Then they built new ships, barges to use on rivers and vessels to use at sea. Last not least they had to build special trucks to transport the big parts on the road.

Country	Employees
Germany	23,186
France	23,116
United Kingdom	7,361
Spain	7,278
others	2,030
total	62,751

M7 Employees of Airbus S.A.S. (2010)

TASKS

1. Make a fact sheet about the A380 in German.
2. Explain why the Airbus A380 is a European aeroplane for the world.
3. Imagine you were able to watch the transport of Airbus components in the south of France. Write an exciting report about it in English or German.

KEY TERMS

- aeroplane
- company
- component
- employee
- final assembly
- manufacturing site
- plant
- port
- supply company

www.airbus.com

M1 Edinburgh's inner city

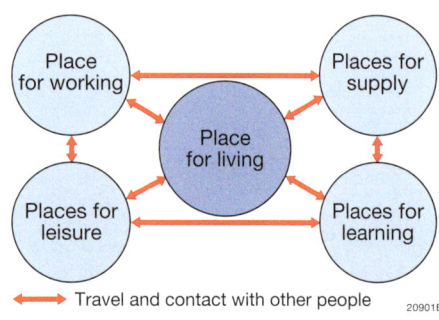

M2 All people need places

A Working Day in Edinburgh

Bonnie McPherson is 19 years old. She lives in a flat in Sighthill on the outskirts of Edinburgh, the capital of Scotland. She works in a bank in the inner city (New Town). She travels to and from work by bus.

Twice a week she learns Italian in a language school. Sometimes she meets friends after work in one of the pubs in Edinburgh's Old Town.

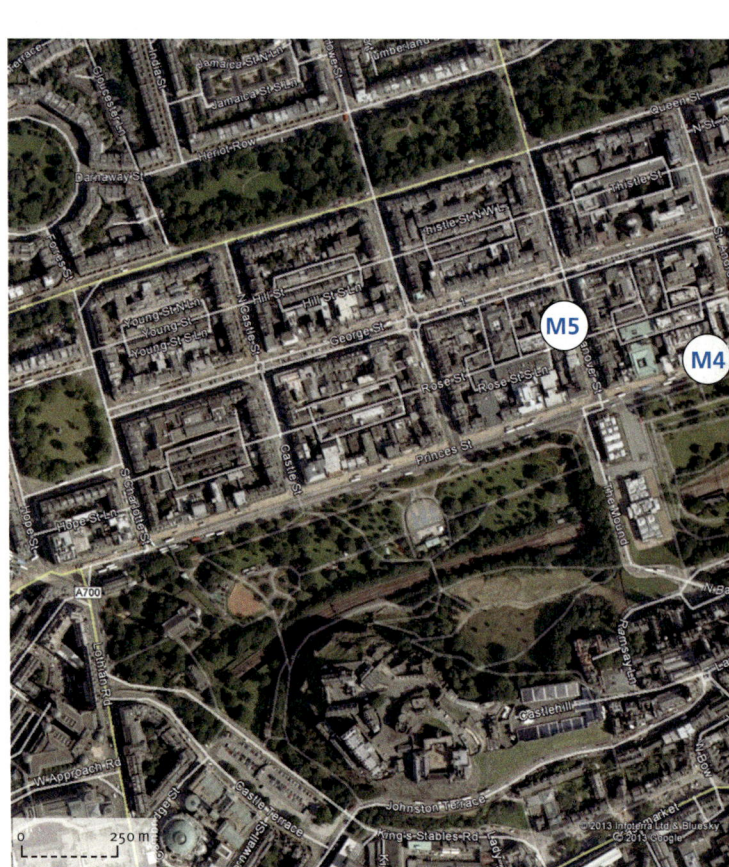

M3 Satellite image of Edinburgh's inner city

M4 Shopping in Princes Street

Germany and Europe

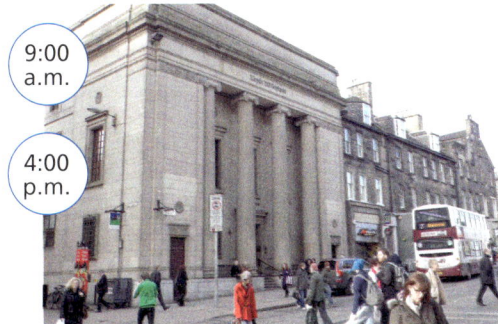

M5 Bank in Hanover Street

M7 Bus stop in Princes Street

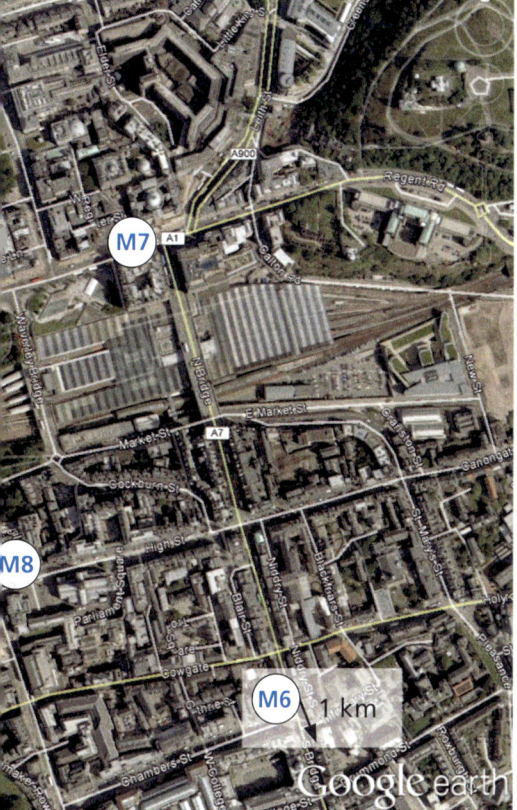

TASKS

1. Draw a sketch of **M2** in your exercise book and translate it into German.
2. Describe Bonnie's day in Edinburgh in writing. The time tags next to the photos and the key terms will help you.
3. Describe your own working day with the help of **M2**.

KEY TERMS

- inner city
- leisure
- outskirts
- supply
- travel
- working day

HELPFUL WORDS AND PHRASES

for TASK 2:
- In the morning / at lunchtime / in the afternoon / in the evening ...
- ... at eight twenty-five a.m. ...
- She arrives at ... (location) ... at ... (time).
- From there she goes to ...
- It is only a short distance ...
- It is a long way to go to ...

M6 Language School in Bernard Terrace

M8 Pub in Lawnmarket

M1 Living on the outskirts

M3 Superstore in the outer city

Living in Edinburgh

Edinburgh is a very popular city. The quality of life is high because job opportunities are good and schools and universities have a very high standard. Although there are no undergrounds, the public transport by trams and buses reaches all parts of the city and its suburbs. The shopping facilities are good, the prices are moderate compared to other cities in the UK. Moreover, Edinburgh offers many leisure activities for the about 850,000 people living in the urban area. So it is not surprising that more and more people want to live there. Edinburgh is the second biggest tourist attraction of the United Kingdom. Old Town and New Town are a UNESCO world heritage site. The famous Edinburgh Festival is the biggest arts festival in the world. It lasts nearly a month throughout August each year.

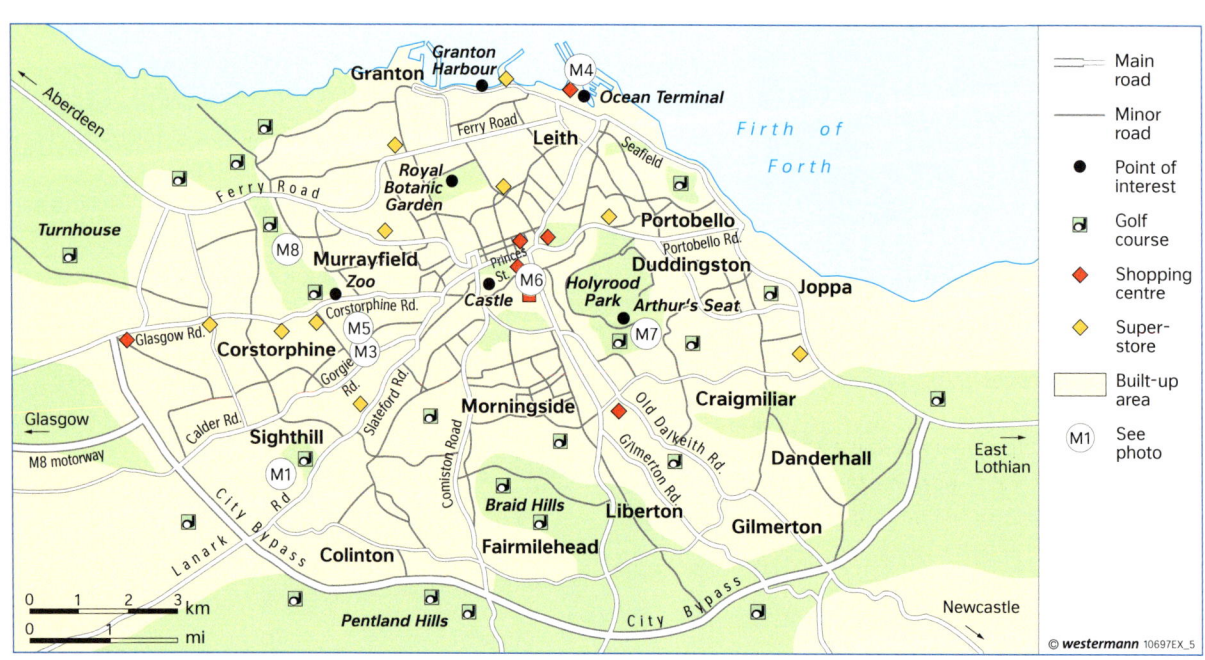
M2 Thematic map of Edinburgh

M4 Ocean Terminal leisure and shopping centre

M5 Murrayfield – home of Scottish rugby

M6 Edinburgh Festival Fringe

A weekend in Edinburgh

Bonnie McPherson looks forward to the weekend. In her free time she likes hiking and playing golf.

Her boyfriend Craig works in the tourist office, so he knows about all the entertainment you can find in Edinburgh. He loves watching rugby. At the weekends he can sometimes get the car of his parents.

They both like going shopping and enjoy cooking together.

M7 View of Arthur's Seat

M8 Golf – a popular leisure activity

TASKS

① a) With the help of the photos, plan a perfect weekend for Bonnie and Craig.
  b) For experts: Calculate the distances they will travel at this weekend.
② Explain why people like to live in Edinburgh.
③ Bonnie and Craig want to visit you. Suggest what they can do in your area.

KEY TERMS

- city
- job opportunity
- leisure activity
- outskirts
- public transport
- shopping facilities
- suburb
- tourist attraction
- urban area

HELPFUL WORDS AND PHRASES

for TASK 1 and TASK 3:
- On Saturday / Sunday morning / noon / afternoon / evening…
- In the morning /afternoon / evening / at noon …
- They walk / drive (from …) to …
- After that … / Later …
- … picks up … from …

M1 In a travel agency

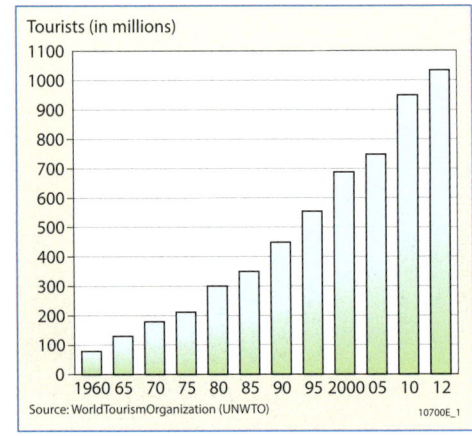

M3 Development of global tourism

The Many Sides of Tourism

What is tourism?

When you spend your holidays away from home, you are one of over one billion tourists who travel the world each year.

Travelling has become easy because cars, trains and aeroplanes allow people to reach regions far away. Travel agencies help tourists to find attractive places all over the world. Most people, however, book their holidays on the Internet where they can compare prices and read about the experiences of other travellers.

Package tours / Individual tourism

Tourists often book package tours which include transport, accommodation and leisure activities. Everything will be organized by the tour operator. A tourist guide at your holiday destination will help you in case of problems. Many people like to book their journey, their accommodation, and their activities separately. This gives them more choices and they sometimes save money that way. These people mostly travel alone or in small groups. Therefore it is called individual tourism.

M2 Low cost carriers at Berlin airport

M4 Tourists in Costa Rica in March

M5 Quad biking in the Alps in December

M7 Sightseeing in New York City/USA in September

M8 Beach in Mar del Plata/Argentina in January

Mass tourism

More and more people look for low-price travels to nice places for their holidays. There they hope to find relaxation, sunshine, and entertainment. The few places where you can find all this within easy reach are very popular.

When many people want to enjoy their holidays in the same place at the same time, it leads to mass tourism. All these tourists need transport, accommodation, and leisure activities.

In the resorts of mass tourism, people find accommodation often in high-rise buildings, very often together with amenities like swimming pools and playgrounds. Bars, restaurants, discotheques and shopping facilities are nearby.

When many people come together in a small area there are often environmental problems with noise, waste, and the destruction of the landscape. On the other hand mass tourism is an important service industry with many jobs.

M6 Amusement park in California in July

TASKS

1. Create a mind map in German, with 'tourism' in its centre, using all the key terms.
2. Compare your mind map in a group of four. Agree on a poster of the mind map in English to show in class.
3. Use M4 to M8 to tell what kind of holiday you like best and what kind you do not like.

KEY TERMS

- accommodation
- amusement park
- individual tourism
- leisure activities
- low-cost carrier
- mass tourism
- package tour
- resort
- service industry
- sightseeing
- tourism
- travel agency

M1 Hiking in the Alps

Holidays in the Alps

The Alps are one of Europe's most famous holiday regions. The tourists not only enjoy the beautiful landscape but also the many different activities they can do throughout the year. This means not only skiing in the winter and hiking in the summer.

The holiday destinations offer exciting attractions like freestyle skiing, free climbing or summer tobogganing (M4). So it is no surprise that more and more tourists come to the Alps every year. The resorts always have something new to attract the tourists.

Too many tourists, however, can cause environmental problems. There have to be new sites for tourist accommodation, for transport, and for tourist attractions. This can spoil the beautiful landscape. There is also a higher risk of avalanches, rockfalls, and mudslides after tourists damage the vegetation (M6).

Many people in the Alps work in the tourist industry and are happy that most hotels and guesthouses are open all year.

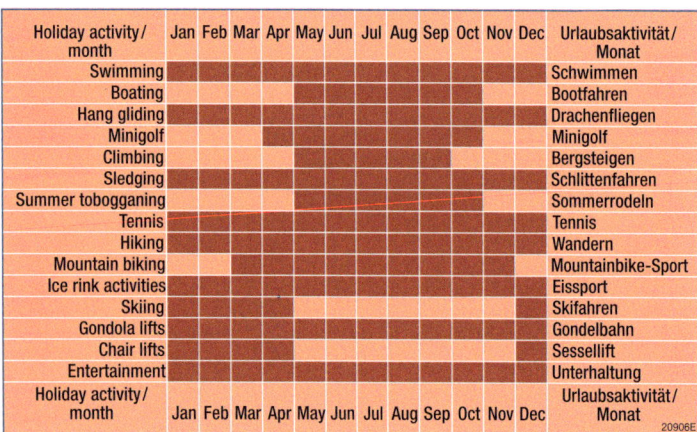

M2 Activities in an alpine holiday resort

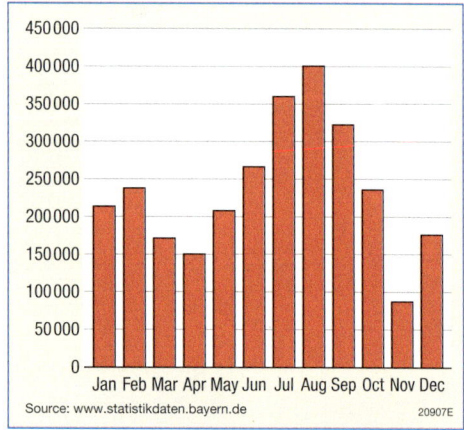

M3 Overnight stays in the Garmisch-Partenkirchen district (2006-2012)

M4 Summer tobogganing

TASKS

1. Explain why the Alps are a famous tourist attraction.
2. Make a list in German, which facilities and which jobs are necessary to offer the resort activities (M2) over the year.
3. Describe the environmental problems which tourism can cause in the Alps.

KEY TERMS

- environmental problem
- hiking
- holiday destination
- holiday region
- holiday season
- skiing
- tourist attraction
- tourist industry

HELPFUL WORDS AND PHRASES

for M2:
- You can do hiking all year long.
- From April to October you can play minigolf.
- You cannot go mountain biking from December to February because …
- Summer is the time to go climbing.

for M3:
- The bar graph shows …
- Overnight stay means that …
- There are more than / less than / over / just under … overnight stays in the G.-P. district in …
- The most / least overnight stays …
- During the winter / spring / summer / autumn (months) there are more / less overnight stays than in …

M5 Ski slope in winter

M6 Ski slope in summer

Malta – A Famous Tourist Place

Legend:
- Built-up area
- Places of interest
- Tourist attraction (Xlendi)
- Beach and sandy beach
- Water sport
- Harbour
- Ferry connection

FACT SHEET

Country profile Malta

Official name:	Repubblika ta' Malta (Maltese) / Republic of Malta (English)
Population:	421,000
Capital:	Valletta (6,000)
Land area:	316 km²; Eight islands, biggest: Malta, Gozo, Comino
Languages:	Maltese, English
Early history:	• Belonged to Italy, Spain, Arab countries • 1814–1964: British colony • 1964: Independent Republic, Member of the British Commonwealth • 2004 EU membership
Economy:	Every third job in Malta is in the tourist industry (2012: 1.4 million tourists).

M1 Some facts about Malta (2014)

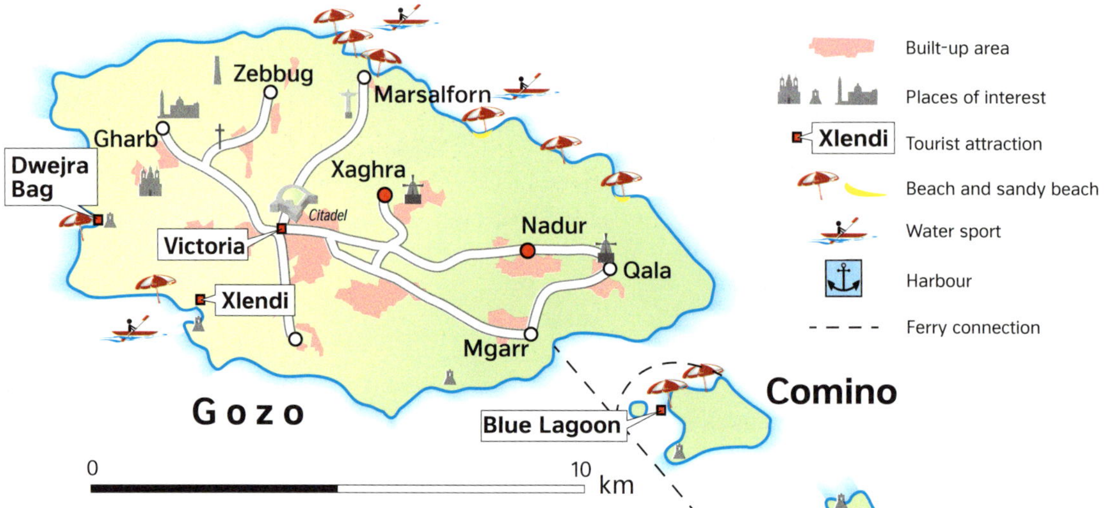

M3 Map of Malta

DE-080 www.diercke.com

	J	F	M	A	M	J	J	A	S	O	N	D	Year
T (°C)	12	13	14	16	19	23	26	26	24	21	18	14	**19**
P (mm)	89	61	39	15	12	2	0	8	29	63	91	110	**519**

M2 Climate data Valletta/Malta (35°54'N / 14°31'E)

M4 Mdina, the former capital

M6 Valletta harbour with yachts

M5 Tourist hotels (St. Julian's Bay)

M7 Seaside holidays on a sandy beach (Qawra)

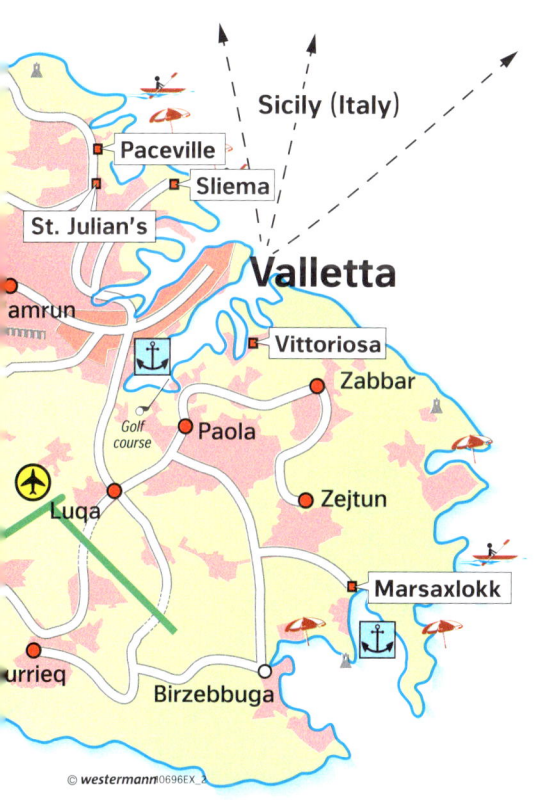

TASKS

1. Turn the Malta fact sheet into a text.
2. Draw a climate graph of Valletta. Explain why this climate favours tourism.
3. Explain why so many people visit Malta for their holidays.
4. Write about your ideal day in a seaside resort in Malta. Use the photos and map for locations.

KEY TERMS

- place of interest
- sandy beach
- seaside holidays
- tourist attraction
- tourist industry

pp. 66-67
Climate Graphs

www.visitmalta.com

HELPFUL WORDS AND PHRASES
for TASK 1:
- ... is altogether ... in size.
- The biggest of ...
- In ... [year] there were ... people living in ...
- From ... until ... Malta was ...
- It became an independent state in ...
- The people in Malta speak ...
- In ... there were ... tourists.
- ... is a very important industry as ... per cent ...

61

How to Work with the Atlas

When you work on the different chapters of your book, you often find tasks which ask you to use your atlas.
The atlas is a collection of many different maps which contain lots of information, the location of places, their height, or economic data, for example.

M2 Two atlases: DIERCKE WELTATLAS / DIERCKE INTERNATIONAL ATLAS

The parts of an atlas

Usually, every atlas has got three parts:

1. The *table of contents* gives you an overview of all the maps that are in your atlas. It tells you the name of the maps and where you can find them.

2. The *collection of maps* is the part that you work with most of the time.

3. The *index* lists all the places that your atlas shows in alphabetical order. Behind the name of the place there is a combination of numbers and letters.

> **HOW TO SAY**
> **...index entries**
>
> The index entry for Mount Rainier in Diercke International Atlas, for example, reads like this:
> *Mount Rainier 138, B2*
>
> Say: 'You can find *Mount Rainier* on page *138* in grid square *B2*.'

How to locate places

... on a map

The *grid square* of a map can help you to find a place that you are looking for. The index entry for a place gives you a page in the atlas and a combination of a letter and a number (B3, for example).

You can find these letters and numbers on the rim of a map, too. Just like in the game of 'Battleships' (**M1**), you can then find the place you are looking for on the map.

M1 Battleships

M3 Map of Northern Germany

... on the global grid

Most maps show the global grid as a set of thin lines with numbers near the rim of the map (› pp. 16-17).

The steps to the right will help you to give the exact location of a place on the global grid. The example is the city Erfurt in Germany.

STEPS

1. Find the line of latitude nearest to Erfurt.
2. Follow this line to the rim of the map and find its number.
3. Do steps 1 and 2 again for the meridian of Erfurt.
4. Write down the location as follows: Latitude / Longitude (Example: Bremen: 53° N / 9° E)

TASKS

1 a) Use your atlas. List the index entries for the following places: Munich, New York City, Mount Everest.
b) List the titles of the maps that show these places.
c) Locate these places on the global grid.

2 Locate Cologne on the global grid with the help of M3.

› p. 17
How to say
... where a place is on the global grid

63

M1 Physical map of Central Europe

How to Read Maps

There are many different kinds of maps in an atlas. They are either physical maps (M1) or thematic maps (M2). Thematic maps can have many different themes. Street maps and road maps are thematic maps, for example. Other thematic maps, which are often used in your atlas, show states and their borders, the economy of a region or country or the population and its characteristics in a region or country.

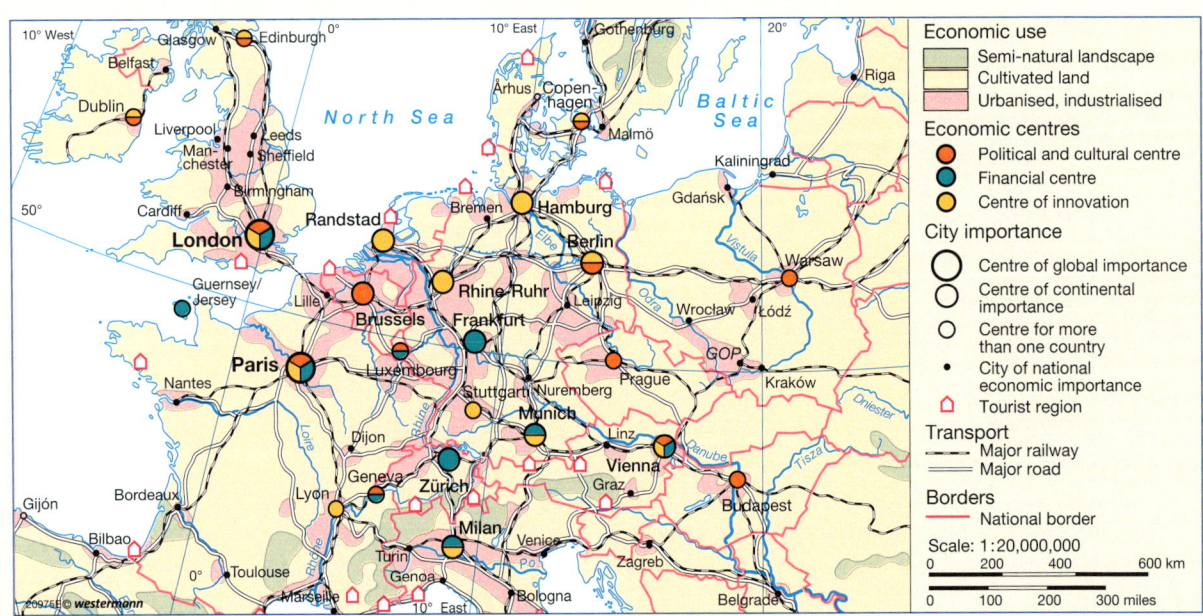

M2 Thematic map of Central Europe

HOW TO SAY ...the scale

Example: Scale 1 : 10,000,000
Say: 'The scale of the map is one to ten million.'

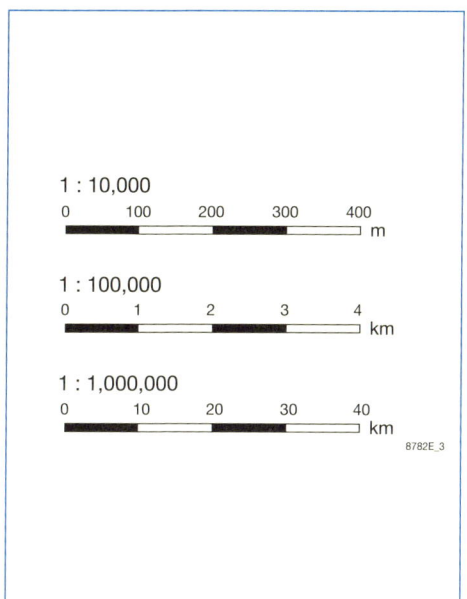

M3 Scale bars

The scale
Smaller numbers behind the colon (1: 10,000) mean big scale. Bigger numbers behind the colon (1: 100,000) mean small scale.

Important parts of maps
Whatever the type of map, there are some features that you can find on every map:

Every map has got a *title*. It often says which part of the world the map shows and what kind of map it is.
Every map has got a *key*. The key of a map tells you what the different colours, lines, and symbols of a map stand for.
Every map has got a *scale*. Map **M1**, for example, has got a scale of 1 : 20,000,000. This means that 1 cm on the map is 20 million centimetres (200 km) in reality. With the help of the scale you can calculate distances. Some maps have got scale bars (**M3**). With a scale bar you can measure distances.

Physical maps
A very important type of map is a physical map. Physical maps always show:
- the height (elevation) of the land above sea level
- the depth of the sea
- the location of rivers, lakes, seas, oceans, and mountains
- the location of cities and borders
- the size of cities

On physical maps the colours green, yellow, and brown show how high the land is. That means that they show the height or elevation of the land.
Be careful: The colour green in physical maps does not mean that there is lots of vegetation!

TASKS

1. Locate the following cities on the global grid with the help of **M1** or **M2**: Prague, Lille, Kiev.
2. Find out the elevation of these cities. Explain how you worked it out.
3. Measure the distance between Berlin and Budapest with the help of the scale bar (**M1** or **M2**).
4. For experts: Calculate the distance between Dublin and Zagreb with the help of the scale.

How to Work with Climate Graphs

How to draw a climate graph

STEPS

1. Take a sheet of squared paper. Draw the base line and divide it into twelve months (1 month ≙ 1 cm).
2. Draw the left axis for the temperature data (10 °C ≙ 1 cm).
3. Draw the right axis for the precipitation data (20 mm ≙ 1 cm). When there are months with a lot of precipitation choose 20, 40, 60, 80, 100, 200, 300 mm and so on.
4. Now draw the blue bars of precipitation for each month.
5. Then make little dots or crosses in the middle of each month for the values of temperature and connect them with a rounded red line.
6. Write down the name of the climate station, the elevation and the position in the grid system at the top of the climate graph.

	J	F	M	A	M	J	J	A	S	O	N	D	Year
(°C)	3.5	3.8	5.7	8.0	11.3	14.4	16.5	16.1	13.8	10.7	6.4	4.5	**9.5**
(mm)	78	51	61	54	55	57	45	56	68	73	77	79	**754**

M1 Climate data of London/United Kingdom (59 m) 51°09′N / 0°11′W

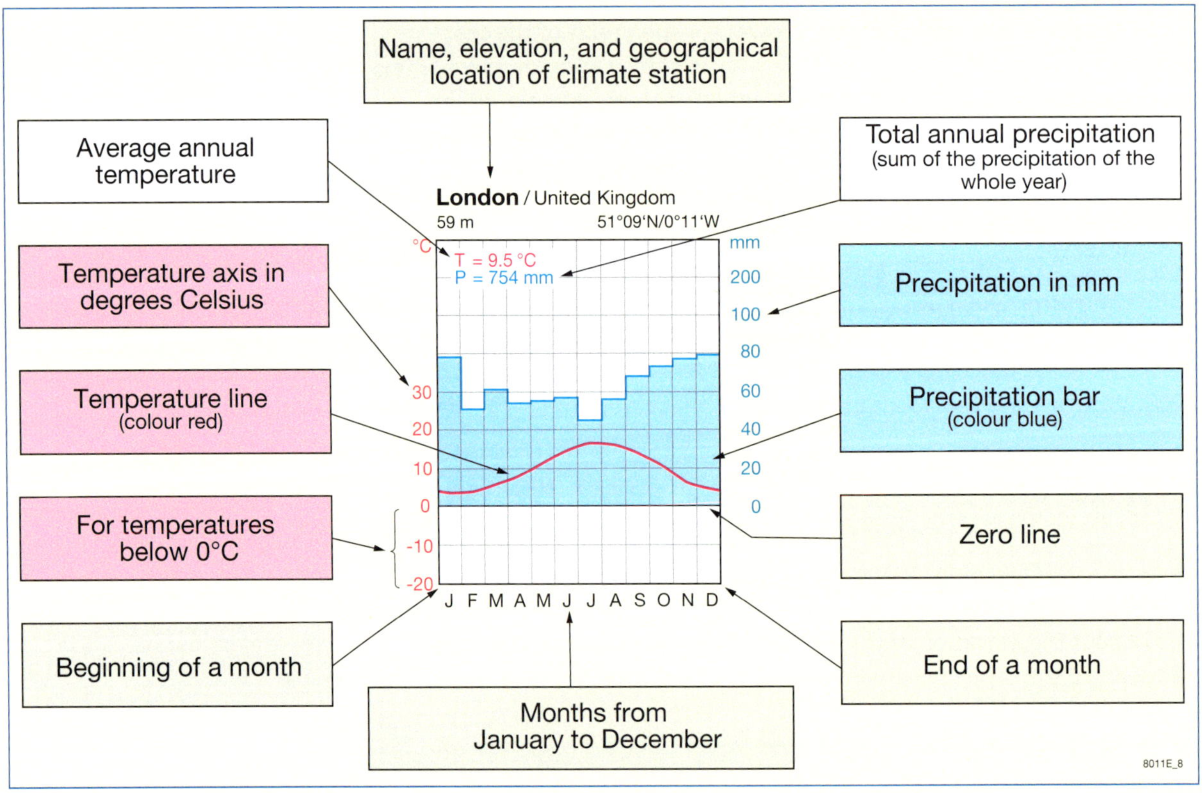

M2 The parts of a climate graph

GEO SKILLS

66

How to describe a climate graph

> **MODEL TEXT ...to describe a climate graph – London (M2)**
>
> 1. The climate station is called London. Its location on the grid system is 51° 09' N and 0°11' W. The station is 59 m above sea level and it is located in the south of the United Kingdom.
> 2. The temperature rises from 3.5 °C in January to 16.5 °C in July. This is a temperature range of 13 °C.
> 3. The driest month is July with a precipitation of 45 mm. The wettest month is December with 79 mm of precipitation. You can say that London has got rainfall throughout the whole year.
> 4. The average temperature is 9.5 °C. The annual precipitation is 754 mm.

	J	F	M	A	M	J	J	A	S	O	N	D	Year
(°C)	−0.4	0.6	4.0	8.4	13.5	16.7	17.9	17.2	13.5	9.3	4.6	1.2	8.9
(mm)	43	37	38	42	55	71	53	65	46	36	50	55	589

M3 Climate data of Berlin/Germany (58 m) 52° 28'N / 13° 18'E

	HELPFUL WORDS AND PHRASES... to describe a climate graph		
1	Start your description with the place name, its location on the grid system, the elevation and a general description of the location.	The climate graph shows the climate of … Its location on the global grid system is … It is located in … … is … m above sea level	
2	As for temperatures, give the months with the highest and lowest temperature. Calculate the temperature range, i.e. the difference between the two.	The maximum / minimum temperature is … The warmest / coldest month(s) is / are … followed by … The temperature range is from …°C to …°C	… rises / increases from … to… … falls / drops from … to …
3	Find out the driest months and the months with the highest amount of precipitation. Look if there is a rainy season or if it rains throughout the whole year.	The maximum / minimum precipitation is … The wettest month(s) is / are …, followed by … The rainy season is …	The dry season is …
4	Finish with the average annual temperature of the year and the total annual precipitation.	The average annual temperature is … The total annual precipitation is …	

TASKS

1 Draw a climate graph of Berlin (**M3**). Describe the climate.

Tasks – Knowing What to Do

When you tackle a task from your book, you have to look out and observe signal words that signal to you what you should do when you answer the task. In German, these signal words are 'Operatoren'.

Signal word	Operator	Was ist zu tun?	Example
Compare / Show the connection between	Vergleiche / Zeige die Verbindung zwischen	Vergleichbares nebeneinander stellen und die Gemeinsamkeiten und Unterschiede herausstellen.	Compare the sizes of the continents.
Describe	Beschreibe	Einen Tatbestand (Tabelle, Graphik) durch umfassende Angaben verständlich machen.	Describe the way of rapeseed oil from the field to the kitchen.
Discuss	Diskutiere	Das Für und Wider bzw. die positiven und negativen Seiten eines Sachverhaltes darstellen und zu einem eigenen Urteil kommen.	Discuss the environmental problems which tourism can cause in the Alps.
Draw a bar graph / climate graph	Zeichne ein Säulendiagramm / Klimadiagramm	Aus Tabellendaten ein Diagramm erstellen.	Draw a climate graph of Valletta.
Draw / Create a mind map	Erstelle eine Mindmap	Ausgehend von einem zentralen Begriff ein Beziehungsgeflecht erstellen.	Draw farmer Fair's business as a mind map.
Draw / Make a table	Zeichne / Erstelle eine Tabelle	Dinge zueinander in Beziehung setzen, indem ein Netz von Zeilen und Spalten erstellt wird.	Make a table about the different climate regions in Europe.
Explain	Erkläre	Durch Darstellen der Ursachen bzw. Zusammenhänge das Verstehen eines Sachverhaltes ermöglichen.	Explain why living in Europe has become easier.
Locate	Verorte	Einen Standort bestimmen (Gradnetz, Atlas).	Locate your home on the global grid.
Make a fact sheet / fact file	Erstelle ein Merkblatt / einen Steckbrief	Die wichtigsten Informationen unter einigen Hauptüberschriften zusammenstellen.	Make a fact sheet about the A380.
Make a list / List	Erstelle eine Liste	Eine knappe, geordnete Zusammenstellung von Fakten in Stichpunkten.	List all landlocked countries.
Match	Ordne zu	Gemeinsamkeiten unkommentiert darstellen.	Match the seasons and the correct pictures.
Name	Nenne	Informationen unkommentiert wiedergeben.	Name the advantages of oilseed rape farming.
Prepare and give a talk / presentation	Bereite einen Vortrag / eine Präsentation vor und halte ihn (sie).	Siehe „Treppe"	Prepare and give a talk about one renewable energy in a group of three.
Record	Zeichne auf	In passender Form Beobachtungsergebnisse sammeln.	Record the precipitation.

General remarks

1. Give your answer a structure. Tasks which ask you to produce a text should have:
   a) a short *introduction*,
   b) the *main part* of the answer to the task, and
   c) a *summary* which could repeat the most important aspects of your answer.
2. Use geographical terms, which often are key words of the topic.
3. Use your own wording, do not just copy the text from the book or other sources. Using your own words shows that you really thought about the task and found your own solution.
4. To describe a table or a graph, never describe the figures, always describe the facts represented by the figures. Do not say, for example, 'the graph rises' – rather say 'the temperature rises'. Do not say 'the figures doubled' – rather say 'the number of passengers doubled'.

Helpful words when you make and describe graphic organizers (tables and graphs):

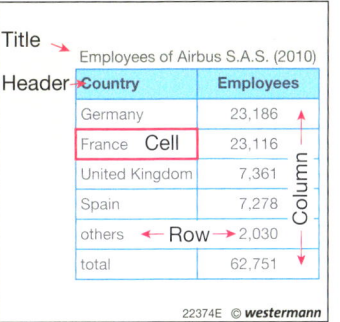

M1 Table

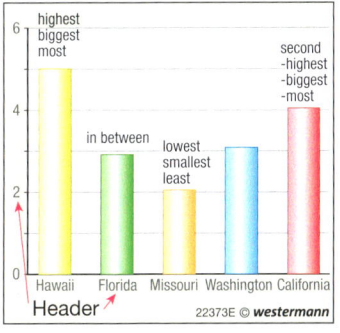

M2 Bar graph

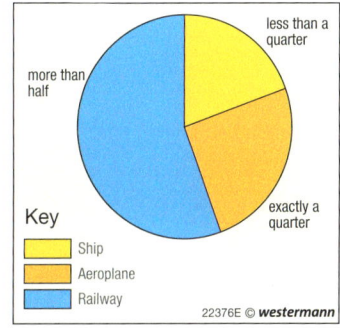

M3 Line graph

M4 Pie chart

Four steps to a good presentation

4. GIVE YOUR TALK
Speak slowly and loudly. Use your notes to support yourself. Enjoy your presentation.

3. PREPARE THE PRESENTATION
Note down keywords for the oral report. Prepare sketches, diagrams etc. Make it interesting, motivating (how can I make everybody listen?). Practise your talk.

2. ORGANISE THE MATERIAL
Decide on importance, find the main points, give a structure and outline.

1. BECOME AN EXPERT
Collect information, study texts, diagrams, tables, photos etc.

Words

A
accommodation Unterkunft
aeroplane Flugzeug
to **affect** beeinträchtigen, beeinflussen
agribusiness Agrobusiness
agriculture Landwirtschaft
all over the world weltweit
although obwohl
amenities Annehmlichkeiten
amount of Höhe, Menge von
amusement park Freizeitpark
anemometer Anemometer/Windmesser
arable farming Ackerbau
area Fläche
to **attract** anlocken
avalanche Lawine
average durchschnittlich, Durchschnitt
    The average annual temperature of … is … °C.
axis Achse
    … spins on its axis. / The axis is tilted.

B
barge Binnenschiff
below unter
between zwischen
biomass energy Energie aus Biomasse
body of water Gewässer
border Grenze
    at the English border
to **breathe** atmen
built-up area überbaute Fläche

C
cache geheimes Lager
to **calculate** berechnen
to **call** nennen
capital Hauptstadt
    The capital of a country…
to **capture** einfangen
to **cause** bedingen, verursachen
certain bestimmte
chapter Kapitel
characteristics Merkmale
to **circle** kreisen
city Stadt
climate Klima
cloudy bewölkt
    cloudy sky / it is cloudy
coastline Küstenlinie
cold kalt
collection Sammlung
company Unternehmen
to **compare** vergleichen
    Compare the size of the oceans to / with the size of the continents.
component Einzelteil
to **connect** verbinden
    The railway connects A to / with B.
connection Verbindung
to **contain** beinhalten
content Inhalt
continent Kontinent
continental climate Kontinentalklima
contract farming Vertragsanbau
cool kühl
costly teuer
to **cover** bedecken
crop Feldfrucht/Nutzpflanze
    Farmers grow lots of differents crops: wheat and corn, for example.
crude oil Rohöl
cube Würfel
currency Währung
customs Zoll(behörde)
    … to pay customs / to pass through customs …

D
dairy farming Milchviehhaltung
to **damage** beschädigen
darkness Dunkelheit
data Daten
daytime Tageszeit, Tageslicht
    during daytime
to **deal** beschäftigen
    to deal with something
degree Grad
dense dicht
depth Tiefe
to **describe** beschreiben
desert Wüste
destination Ziel, Bestimmungsort
destruction Zerstörung
device Gerät
difference Unterschied
different unterschiedlich, anders
direction Richtung, hier: Himmelsrichtung
to **divide** teilen
dot Punkt
to **draw** zeichnen
to **drill** bohren
driving licence Führerschein
dry trocken

E
Earth Erde
Earth's axis Erdachse
economic data Wirtschaftsdaten
economy Wirtschaft
elevation Erhebung, Höhe
employee Angestellte(r)
entertainment Unterhaltung
entry Eintrag
environmental problem Umweltproblem
Equator Äquator
European transportation network Europäisches Transportnetzwerk

European Union Europäische Union
to exchange wechseln, umtauschen
experience Erfahrung
to explain erklären
to extract fördern

F

to face begegnen
to farm anbauen, Ackerbau betreiben
facilities Einrichtungen, Anlagen
to fail versagen
farming type landwirtschaftlicher Betriebstyp
feature Eigenschaft
ferry connection Fährverbindung
fertile soil fruchtbarer Boden
fertilizer Dünger
final assembly Endfertigung
finished product Fertigware, Endprodukt
fly-fishing Fliegenfischen
to follow folgen
forecast Vorhersage
    a weather forecast for tomorrow
to furnish einrichten

G

geothermal energy Energie aus Erdwärme
gentle sanft
global grid Gradnetz der Erde
    The position of X on the global grid is 50° S and 127° W.
globe Globus
    around the globe / surface of the globe
goods Güter
to go on holiday Urlaub machen
to go shopping Einkaufen gehen, shoppen
GPS (Global Positioning System)
    Globales Navigationssystem
to graze weiden
grid Gitter
grid square Planquadrat
    Birmingham is in grid square C4.
to grow (wachsen), anbauen
    Lots of the farmers grow wheat and corn.
to grow something etwas anbauen
growth Wachstum

H

to harvest ernten
heat Hitze
height Höhe
hemisphere Halbkugel
    India is in the Northern Hemisphere.
to hide verstecken
hiking Wandern
hill farming Berglandwirtschaft
hilly area hügelige Landschaft
hint Hinweis

to hold on to something sich an etwas festhalten
holiday destination Reiseziel
holiday region Urlaubsregion
holiday season Urlaubssaison
hot heiß
huge enorm, sehr groß
    a huge amount of / a huge country
hydroelectric energy Energie aus Wasserkraft
hydrogen fuel cells Brennstoffzellen

I

ID-card Pass, Ausweis
image Bild
to improve verbessern
in detail ausführlich
in fact tatsächlich
    In fact, London is bigger than Berlin.
in the course of im Verlauf
include einschließen
individual tourism Individualtourismus
to influence beeinflussen
inhabitants Einwohner
    inhabitants of England
inner city Innenstadt
insurance Versicherung
International Date Line Internationale Datumsgrenze
    crossing the International Date Line
invisible unsichtbar

J

job opportunities Beschäftigungs-möglichkeiten

L

to label beschriften, benennen
landlocked country Binnenstaat
landmass Landmasse
landscape Landschaft
language Sprache
large groß
    a large country / larger than Germany
to last (an-)dauern
leisure (time) Freizeit
leisure activities Freizeitaktivitäten
line of latitude Breitengrad
line of longitude Längengrad
to link verbinden, vernetzen
to locate orten, verorten
to be located sich befinden
    Berlin is located in the east of Germany.
location Ort
logistics industry Logistikbranche
to look forward to sich freuen auf
low-cost carrier Billigflieger

M

maize Mais
maker Hersteller
manioc Maniok
manufacturing industry Produzierendes Gewerbe
manufacturing site Produktionsstätte
maritime climate maritimes Klima
market gardening Erwerbsgartenbau
mass tourism Massentourismus
matter Stoff
to **measure** messen
meat Fleisch
Mediterranean climate mediterranes Klima
to **meet** sich treffen
member Mitglied
    member states / the member of …
meridian Meridian
mild mild
millet Hirse
mining Bergbau
moderate gemäßigt
moon Mond
mountainous area bergige Landschaft
mudslide Schlammlawine, Mure

N

natural gas Erdgas
neighbouring benachbart
    neighbouring country
nighttime Nachtzeit, Dunkelheit
non-renewable resource nicht erneuerbare Ressource
North Pole Nordpol
    beneath the North Pole
Northern Hemisphere nördliche Hemisphäre
to **number** nummerieren
number plate Nummernschild, Autokennzeichen

O

oblique rays schräg einfallende Strahlen
    Oblique rays heat up…
ocean Ozean
to **offer** anbieten
offshore oil platform (oil rig) Ölbohrinsel
oil spill Ölunfall
oil terminal Ölterminal
oilseed rape Raps
one in … (fifteen) einer von … (fünfzehn)
on offer verfügbar
outskirts Stadtrand, Außenbezirke
overview Überblick

P

package tour Pauschalreise
parliament Parlament
to **pass** überschreiten, passieren
passport Reisepass
permanently ständig
pipeline Pipeline, Rohrleitung
place of interest Sehenswürdigkeit
plain Ebene, flaches Land
plant Produktionsanlage, Fabrik
to **plough** pflügen
points of the compass Himmelsrichtungen
poisonous giftig
polar region Polarregion
to **pollute** verschmutzen
poor soil unfruchtbarer Boden
popular beliebt
population Bevölkerung
port Hafen
power station Kraftwerk
precipitation Niederschlag
    Rain is a type of precipitation.
primary sector Primärer Sektor
Prime Meridian Nullmeridian
public transport Öffentlicher Verkehr (ÖPNV)
put off abschrecken

Q

quaternary industry Quartärer Wirtschaftszweig

R

rain gauge Niederschlagsmesser
rainy regnerisch
raw material Rohstoff
receiver Empfänger
refinery Raffinerie
relatively relativ, verhältnismäßig
    it is relatively dry / humid
relaxation Entspannung
relief Relief
religion Religion
renewable energy Erneuerbare Energie
renewable resource Erneuerbare Ressource
reservoir Stausee
resort Urlaubsort
revolution Umdrehung
    Earth's revolution around the sun. / The Earth revolves around the sun.
rickshaw Rikscha
rim Rand
to **rise up** aufsteigen, ansteigen
risk Gefahr
rock fall Felssturz
roof Dach
run through verlaufen durch, durchlaufen
    the border runs through the Mediterranean Sea
run out enden

S

sandy beach Sandstrand
satellite image Satellitenbild
screen Bildschirm
seaside holidays Urlaub am Meer
season Jahreszeit

secondary sector   Sekundärer Sektor
to **separate**   trennen
separately   getrennt
service industry   Dienstleistungen
sewage   Abwasser
shade   Schatten
shopping facilities   Einkaufsmöglichkeiten
short   kurz
to **show**   zeigen
sightseeing   Besichtigung, Sightseeing
site   Stätte
to be **situated**   gelegen sein
   London is situated in the south-east of England.
size   Größe
skiing   Skifahren
small   klein
soil   Boden
solar energy   Solarenergie
solar system   Sonnensystem
source   Quelle
South Pole   Südpol
   At the Southpole ...
Southern Hemisphere   südliche Hemisphäre
   On the Southern Hemisphere ...
to **sow**   säen
sparse   karg, spärlich
to **spend**   verbringen
   to spend one`s holidays
to **spin**   drehen
   to spin on an axis
split off   (sich) abspalten
spoil   verunzieren, verderben
square   Quadrat
staff   Beschäftigte(r)
state   Staat
steep   steil
   a steep mountain
step   Schritt
suburb   Vorort
suitable   geeignet
Sun   Sonne
sunny   sonnig
supply   Versorgung
supply company   Zulieferfirma
surface   Oberfläche
   on the surface
surprise   Überraschung

T

tag   Kennzeichen, Tag
temperature   Temperatur
temperature range   Temperaturbereich
   temperature range from...°C to ...°C
tertiary sector   Tertiärer Sektor
than   als
   smaller / bigger / hotter than ...
that way   auf diese Weise
thermometer   Thermometer
there is   es gibt
through   durch
throughout the year   über das Jahr hinweg

tidal energy   Gezeitenenergie
tide(s)   Gezeiten
tilt   Neigung, Neigungswinkel
   to have a tilt
time difference   Zeitunterschied, Zeitverschiebung
time zone   Zeitzone
tour operator   Reiseveranstalter
tourism   Tourismus
tourist attraction   Touristenattraktion
tourist guide   Reiseführer
tourist industry   Touristikbranche
tram   Straßenbahn
transitional climate   Übergangsklima
travel   Reise
travel   reisen, unterwegs sein
   to travel the world / to travel by bus
travel agency   Reisebüro
treasure   Schatz
treasure hunter   Schatzsucher
treasure hunting   Schatzsuche
tropical rainforest   Tropischer Regenwald
truck   Lkw

U

underground   U-Bahn
UNESCO world heritage site   UNESCO Welterbestätte
upland   Hochland
urban area   Städtischer Raum
to **use**   benutzen

V

vegetation   Vegetation
   There is dense vegetation in tropical rainforests.
vertical rays   senkrecht einfallende Strahlen
   Vertical rays reach ...
vessel   Schiff
village   Dorf

W

warehouse   Lagerhalle
waste   Abfall
wave energy   Wellenenergie
weather   Wetter
   How is the weather? / The weather is / was rainy...
weather elements   Wetterelemente
weather map   Wetterkarte
   ...on the weather map / The weather map shows...
weather station   Wetterstation
wet   nass, feucht
wind direction   Windrichtung
   main wind direction
wind energy   Windenergie
wind speed   Windstärke
windsock   Windsack
windy   windig
within easy reach   leicht zu erreichen
work   Arbeit

Glossary

A

accommodation [əˌkɒmə'deɪʃ(ə)n], p. 57
Unterkunft – Lodgings in a house or similar living quarters that are given to travellers in hotels or on cruise ships.

aeroplane ['eərəˌpleɪn], p. 51
Flugzeug – Fixed-wing machine that can fly and is heavier than air.

agribusiness ['ægrɪˌbɪznəs], p. 43
Agrobusiness – Farming on a large scale, often combining the growing and marketing of farm produce.

agriculture ['ægrɪˌkʌltʃə(r)], p. 41
Landwirtschaft – Cultivation of arable land. This includes → crop, fruit, and seed growing and horticulture, as well as livestock farming and → dairy farming.

amusement park [ə'mju:zmənt pɑː(r)k], p. 57
Freizeitpark – Entertainment attractions, rides, and other events in a location for the enjoyment of large numbers of people.

anemometer [ænɪ'mɒmətə], p. 25
Anemometer/Windmesser – An instrument for measuring the speed of wind. The cups of the anemometer spin around. The number of revolutions in a given time gives the wind speed.

arable farming ['ærəb(ə)l 'fɑː(r)mɪŋ], p. 41
Ackerbau – Growing of → crops on farms.

axis ['æksɪs], p. 15
Achse – see → Earth's axis.

B

biomass energy ['baɪəʊˌmæs 'enə(r)dʒi], p. 47
Energie aus Biomasse – Sustainable energy gained from animal and plant matter through burning or fuel production.

body of water ['bɒdi ɒv 'wɔːtə(r)], p. 11
Gewässer – Accumulations of water on the surface of the → Earth, such as → oceans, seas, lakes, ponds, rivers, streams, and canals.

border ['bɔː(r)də(r)], p. 35
Grenze – Line separating two systems, either man-made (e.g. → states) or natural (e.g. plates).

C

capital ['kæpɪt(ə)l], p. 31, 35
Hauptstadt – City with the seat of government.

city ['sɪti], p. 55
(Groß-)Stadt – Concentration of people and buildings with an inner central business district and → outskirts where most people live.

climate ['klaɪmət], p. 27
Klima – Average → weather conditions of a certain region over at least 30 years.

company ['kʌmp(ə)ni], p. 51
Unternehmen – Business for production or services.

component [kəm'pəʊnənt], p. 51
Einzelteil – Part that can be put together with others to produce a functioning unit.

continent ['kɒntɪnənt], p. 11
Kontinent – Very large land area surrounded by → oceans.

continental climate [ˌkɒntɪ'nent(ə)l 'klaɪmət], p. 39
Kontinentalklima – → Climate with high → temperature range between warm summers and cold winter.

contract farming ['kɒntrækt 'fɑː(r)mɪŋ], p. 43
Vertragsanbau – Employment of specialised firms for specific farming activities on a contract basis.

crop [krɒp], p. 27, 43
Feldfrucht/Nutzpflanze – Cultivated plant, especially a cereal, fruit, or vegetable.

crude oil [kruːd ɔɪl], p. 45
Rohöl – Primary energy resource, also called petroleum, found in deposits in the → Earth's crust. It is the basic raw material for the production of petrol, kerosene, light oil, etc.

customs ['kʌstəmz], p. 37
Zoll(behörde) – The place (e.g. at a → border or an airport) that checks which goods one brings into a country.

D

dairy farming ['deɪri 'fɑː(r)mɪŋ], p. 41
Milchviehhaltung – Rearing of cows for milk production.

daytime ['deɪˌtaɪm], p. 15
Tageszeit, Tageslicht – Time of day when the sky is lit by the → Sun.

desert ['dezə(r)t], p. 27
Wüste – Dry zone covered with rock, gravel or sand, but only sparse → vegetation.

E

Earth [ɜː(r)θ], p. 7
Erde – → Planet on which we live. 3rd planet in the → solar system.

Earth's axis [ɜː(r)θs 'æksɪs], p. 21
Erdachse – Imaginary line running from the → North Pole to the → South Pole the → Earth spins around.

employee [ɪmˈplɔɪiː], p. 51
Angestellte(r) – Person with a job in a → company or in civil services.

environmental problem
[ɪnˌvaɪrənˈment(ə)l ˈprɒbləm], p. 59
Umweltproblem/Umweltschaden – Damage to the environment caused by human activities.

Equator [ɪˈkweɪtə(r)], p. 17
Äquator – Longest → line of latitude with an equal distance from the two poles, dividing the → Northern and Southern Hemisphere.

Euro [ˌjʊərəˈ], p. 37
Euro (Währung) – Most members of the European Union have introduced a common currency, the Euro.

European transportation network
[ˌjʊərəˈpiːən ˌtrænspɔː(r)ˈteɪʃ(ə)n ˈnetˌwɜː(r)k], p. 37
Europäisches Transportnetzwerk – A network of e.g. roads and railways that connect different parts of Europe.

European Union [ˌjʊərəˈpiːən ˈjuːnjən], p. 37
Europäische Union – An economic and political organization that many European countries belong to.

F

farming type [ˈfɑː(r)mɪŋ taɪp], p. 41
landwirtschaftlicher Betriebstyp – Classification of farms, depending on production (e.g. → dairy farming), ownership (e.g. family farm) or market orientation (e.g. subsistence farming).

final assembly [ˈfaɪn(ə)l əˈsembli], p. 51
Endfertigung – Last step in a production line in which all → components are put together.

forecast [ˈfɔː(r)kɑːst], p. 23
Vorhersage – A description of what something (e.g. the weather) will be like in the future.

G

gas terminal [gæs ˈtɜː(r)mɪn(ə)l], p. 45
Gasterminal – see → oil terminal.

geothermal energy
[ˌdʒiːəʊˈθɜː(r)m(ə)l ˈenə(r)dʒi], p. 47
Energie aus Erdwärme – Sustainable energy made by heat inside the → Earth's crust.

global grid [ˈgləʊb(ə)l grɪd], p. 17
Gradnetz der Erde – Net of virtual → lines of latitude and longitude with which you can position everything on → Earth.

globe [gləʊb], p. 15
Globus – → Earth as a whole. Also: A small 3-D model of it.

GPS (Global Positioning System) [ˌdʒiː piː ˈes, (ˈgləʊb(ə)l pəˈzɪʃ(ə)nɪŋ ˈsɪstəm)], p. 17
Globales Navigationssystem – Signals from satellites are used to show the exact location of a person or thing on Earth through a special device.

H

hemisphere [ˈhemɪˌsfɪə(r)], p. 17, 21
Halbkugel – One half of the → Earth, either divided along the Equator (→ Northern and Southern H.) or by the → Prime Meridian and 180° meridian (Eastern and Western H.).

hiking [ˈhaɪkɪŋ], p. 59
Wandern – Travelling on foot in the mountains or the countryside.

hill farming [hɪl ˈfɑː(r)mɪŋ], p. 41
Berglandwirtschaft – Farming in a → mountainous area. The prevailing grassland is mainly used for cattle or sheep grazing.

hilly area [ˈhɪli ˈeəriə], p. 33
hügelige Landschaft – An area with a lot of hills.

holiday destination
[ˈhɒlɪdeɪ ˌdestɪˈneɪʃ(ə)n], p. 59
Reiseziel – Area or place where people go to on their holidays.

holiday region [ˈhɒlɪdeɪ ˈriːdʒ(ə)n], p. 59
Urlaubsregion – Area which is popular for tourists to spend their holidays in.

holiday season [ˈhɒlɪdeɪ ˈsiːz(ə)n], p. 59
Urlaubssaison – Time in which many people take their holidays.

hydroelectric energy
[ˌhaɪdrəʊɪˈlektrɪk ˈenə(r)dʒi], p. 47
Energie aus Wasserkraft – Sustainable energy created by flowing water.

hydrogen fuel cell
[ˈhaɪdrədʒən ˈfjuːəl sel], p. 47
Brennstoffzelle – Converts hydrogen into electricity by chemically mixing it with oxygen, from which results water. They are like batteries that are constantly fed with fuel.

I

individual tourism
[ˌɪndɪˈvɪdʒuəl ˈtʊərɪz(ə)m], p. 57
Individualtourismus – Travel organised and carried out on an individual basis or in small groups.

inhabitant [ɪnˈhæbɪtənt], p. 13, 31
Einwohner – Person living in a particular place (e.g. city or country).

inner city [ˈɪnə(r) ˈsɪti], p. 53
Innenstadt – Area of a town or a → city which is the centre of administration, shopping, business and entertainment.

International Date Line
[ˌɪntə(r)ˈnæʃ(ə)nəl deɪt laɪn], p. 19
Internationale Datumsgrenze – Imaginary line roughly along the 180° → meridian. West of this line the calendar date is one day ahead of the calendar date east of the line.

J

job opportunity [dʒɒb ˌɒpə(r)ˈtjuːnəti], p. 55
Beschäftigungsmöglichkeit – Chance to get a job.

L

landlocked country [ˈlæn(d)ˌlɒkt ˈkʌntri], p. 35
Binnenstaat – A country that is almost or completely surrounded by land.

landmass [lændmæs], p. 11
Landmasse – Area of land surrounded by an → ocean.

landscape [ˈlæn(d)ˌskeɪp], p. 27
Landschaft – The physical elements of landforms and the living elements, such as → vegetation, in combination with human elements, such as land use, of a certain area.

language [ˈlæŋgwɪdʒ], p. 13
Sprache – Human communication by using spoken or written words.

leisure (time) [ˈleʒə(r) (taɪm)], p. 53
Freizeit – Free time, when a person can choose what to do.

leisure activity [ˈleʒə(r) ækˈtɪvəti], p. 55,57
Freizeitaktivität – Thing you do in your free time.

line of latitude
[laɪn ɒv ˈlætɪˌtjuːd], p. 17
Breitengrad – Set of lines of the global grid. Lines of latitude run from east to west and are labelled north and south.

line of longitude [laɪn ɒv ˈlɒndʒɪˌtjuːd], p. 17
Längengrad – Set of lines of the → global grid. Lines of longitude run from north to south and are labelled east and west. They cross the → North Pole as well as the → South Pole. One half of a line of longitude is called → meridian.

low-cost carrier [ləʊ kɒst ˈkæriə(r)], p. 57
Billigflieger – Airline which tries to keep its prices and fares lower than others, also called a budget airline.

M

manufacturing industry
[ˌmænjʊˈfæktʃərɪŋ ˈɪndəstri], p. 49
Produzierendes Gewerbe – Business of producing goods in factories.

manufacturing site
[ˌmænjʊˈfæktʃərɪŋ saɪt], p. 51
Produktionsstätte – Place or location where goods are produced in factories.

maritime climate [ˈmærɪˌtaɪm ˈklaɪmət], p. 39
maritimes Klima – → Climate with little temperature differences between cool summers and mild winters.

market gardening
[ˈmɑː(r)kɪt ˈgɑː(r)d(ə)nɪŋ], p. 41
Erwerbsgartenbau – Commercial growing of vegetables, salad, flowers, etc., mostly sold in → cities nearby.

mass tourism [mæs ˈtʊərɪz(ə)m], p. 57
Massentourismus – Business of providing services for holiday activities on a large scale.

Mediterranean climate
[ˌmedɪtəˈreɪniən ˈklaɪmət], p. 39
mediterranes Klima – → Climate with warm, dry summers and mild, wet winters.

meridian [məˈrɪdiən], p. 17
Meridian – One half of a → line of longitude. They connect → North Pole and → South Pole.

moon [muːn], p. 7
Mond – Object that goes around a → planet.

mountainous area [ˈmaʊntɪnəs ˈeəriə], p. 33
bergige Landschaft – An area having many mountains.

N

natural gas [ˈnætʃ(ə)rəl gæs], p. 45
Erdgas – Mixture of inflammable gases, mainly methane. Often found together with petroleum.

nighttime [ˈnaɪtˌtaɪm], p. 15
Nachtzeit, Dunkelheit – Period of darkness between evening and morning.

non-renewable resource
[nɒn rɪˈnjuːəb(ə)l rɪˈzɔː(r)s], p. 45
nicht erneuerbare Ressource – Natural resource that is used up faster than it can be made by nature, so there is no more available for future use.

North Pole [nɔː(r)θ pəʊl], p. 15
Nordpol – The northernmost point of the → Earth located at 90° N.

Northern Hemisphere
[ˈnɔː(r)ðə(r)n ˈhemɪˌsfɪə(r)], p. 17, 21
nördliche Hemisphäre – see → Hemisphere.

O

oblique rays [əˈbliːk reɪz], p. 21
schräg einfallende Strahlen – Sun rays that reach the → Earth at an angle of less than 90°.

ocean [ˈəʊʃ(ə)n], p. 11
Ozean – Large water mass between the → continents.

offshore oil platform (oil rig)
[ˌɒfˈʃɔː(r) ɔɪl ˈplætˌfɔː(r)m (ɔɪl rɪg)], p. 45
Ölbohrinsel – Large structure in the sea with facilities to drill wells, to extract and process oil and → natural gas, and to temporarily store them.

oil field [ɔɪl fiːld], p. 45
Ölfeld – Deposits of → crude oil in the → Earth's crust.

oil spill [ɔɪl spɪl], p. 45
Ölunfall – Pollution of the environment with → crude oil or its products.

oil terminal [ɔɪl ˈtɜː(r)mɪn(ə)l], p. 45
Ölterminal – Large industrial complex where oil and → natural gas is stored and from which it is transported elsewhere.

oilseed rape [ˌɔɪlsiːd ˈreɪp], p. 43
Raps – Bright yellow flowering → crop, cultivated mainly for its oil-rich seed.

outskirts [ˈaʊtˌskɜː(r)ts], p. 53, 55
Stadtrand, Außenbezirk – Outlying areas of a → city or town.

P

package tour [ˈpækɪdʒ tʊə(r)], p. 57
Pauschalreise – Tour arranged by a travel agent. Transportation, food, and lodging are all provided at an inclusive price.

parliament [ˈpɑː(r)ləmənt], p. 31
Parlament – Group of people who are elected and manage the political affairs of a country (e.g. the German Bundestag).

pipeline [ˈpaɪpˌlaɪn], p. 45
Pipeline, Rohrleitung – Long tube, used to transport liquids or gases over long distances.

place of interest [pleɪs ɒv ˈɪntrəst], p. 61
Sehenswürdigkeit – Place famous for its scenery or famous historical site.

plain [pleɪn], p. 33
Ebene, flaches Land – An area of flat land.

planet [ˈplænet], p. 7
Planet – Object that goes around the → Sun.

plant [plɑːnt], p. 51
hier: Produktionsanlage, Fabrik – Building or group of buildings for the manufacture of a product, a factory.

points of the compass
[pɔɪnts əv ðiː ˈkʌmpəs], p. 11
Himmelsrichtungen – Mark the directions north, south, east, west.

polar region [ˈpəʊlə(r) ˈriːdʒ(ə)n], p. 27
Polarregion – The areas of the → Earth around the → North Pole and → South Pole.

population [ˌpɒpjʊˈleɪʃ(ə)n], p. 13, 31
Bevölkerung – Total number of people living in a specific area (e.g. settlement of country).

port [pɔː(r)t], p. 51
Hafen – Place on a waterway with facilities for loading and unloading ships.

power station [ˈpaʊə(r) ˈsteɪʃ(ə)n], p. 47
Kraftwerk – Complex of structures and machinery for generating electric energy from another source of energy (e.g. the burning of coal).

precipitation [prɪˌsɪpɪˈteɪʃ(ə)n], p. 23, 27
Niederschlag – Condensed water vapour from the atmosphere which reaches the → surface of the earth as rainfall, dew, hail, snow, fog, etc.

primary sector [ˈpraɪməri ˈsektə(r)], p. 49
Primärer Sektor – Sector of an economy making direct use of natural resources, including → agriculture, forestry and fishing, mining, and extraction of oil and gas.

Prime Meridian [praɪm məˈrɪdiən], p. 17
Nullmeridian – Line of 0° longitude which runs through Greenwich, London. From here the other longitudes from 0° to 180° east, or from 0° to 180° west, are counted.

public transport [ˈpʌblɪk ˈtrænspɔː(r)t], p. 55
Öffentlicher Verkehr (ÖPNV) – System of buses, trains, etc., running on fixed routes, on which the public may travel.

Q

quaternary industry
[ˈkwɒtərˌnɛri ˈɪndəstri], p. 49
Quartärer Wirtschaftszweig – Economic activities mainly concerned with education, research and the media, often still regarded as part of the → tertiary sector.

R

rain gauge [reɪn geɪdʒ], p. 25
Niederschlagsmesser – Measures the amount of → precipitation over a certain period of time in mm.

raw material [rɔː məˈtɪəriəl], p. 45, 49
Rohstoff – Unprocessed material used for the production of goods.

refinery [rɪˈfaɪnəri], p. 45
Raffinerie – Industrial plant for purifying a crude substance, e.g. petroleum or sugar.

relief [rɪˈliːf], p. 27, 33
Relief – Shape of the → Earth's surface.

religion [rɪˈlɪdʒ(ə)n], p. 13, 33
Religion – The belief in the existence of god(s).

renewable energy
[rɪˈnjuːəb(ə)l ˈenə(r)dʒi], p. 47
Erneuerbare Energie – Source of energy which cannot be used up because it is constantly restored, e.g. wind energy.

renewable resource
[rɪˈnjuːəb(ə)l rɪˈzɔː(r)s], p. 43
Erneuerbare Ressource – Any natural resource (e. g. solar energy) that can be replenished naturally with the passage of time. Plants and animals are considered to be renewable resources as well, as long as they are used in a sustainable way.

resort [rɪˈzɔː(r)t], p. 57
Urlaubsort – Place with facilities for people on holiday.

S

sandy beach [ˈsændi biːtʃ], p. 61
Sandstrand – Waterfront for swimming and relaxation made of sand.

seaside holidays [ˈsiːˌsaɪd ˈhɒlɪdeɪɪz], p. 61
Urlaub am Meer – Holidays which are mainly spent on the beach with water activities and sunbathing.

season [ˈsiːz(ə)n], p. 21
Jahreszeit – Period within a year (spring, summer autumn, winter), showing specific natural conditions, which are caused by the duration of daylight, and/or the amount of rainfall (wet season, dry season).

secondary sector [ˈsekənd(ə)r ˈsektə(r)], p. 49
Sekundärer Sektor – Economic activity concerned with the manufacturing of finished products from → raw materials.

service industry [ˈsɜː(r)vɪs ˈɪndəstri], p. 49, 57
Dienstleistungen – Economic activity concerned with the offer of any services, e. g. trade, transport, also known as → tertiary industry.

shopping facilities [ˈʃɒpɪŋ fəˈsɪlətiz], p. 55
Einkaufsmöglichkeit – Any building in which you can buy things.

sightseeing [ˈsaɪtˌsiːɪŋ], p. 57
Besichtigung, Sightseeing – Act or pastime of visiting sights of interest.

skiing [ˈskiːɪŋ], p. 59
Skifahren – Act or sport of gliding on skis.

soil [sɔɪl], p. 41
Boden – Uppermost layer of the → Earth's surface made up of a mixture of weathered rock material, decomposed organic matter, microorganisms, air and water.

solar energy [ˈsəʊlə(r) ˈenə(r)dʒi], p. 47
Solarenergie – Conversion of sunlight to electrical energy, especially in photovoltaic cells.

solar system [ˈsəʊlə(r) ˈsɪstəm], p. 7
Sonnensystem – Sum of the sun, the eight → planets and their → moons.

South Pole [saʊθ pəʊl], p. 15
Südpol – The southernmost point of the → Earth located at 90° S.

Southern Hemisphere
[ˈsʌðə(r)n ˈhemɪˌsfɪə(r)], p. 17, 21
südliche Hemisphäre – see → Hemisphere.

state [steɪt], p. 31
Staat – An independent political unit, e. g. a country. Also: a political unit within a country, such as the 50 states of the USA.

suburb [ˈsʌbɜː(r)b], p. 55
Vorort – Residential district situated on the → outskirts of a → city or town.

Sun [sʌn], p. 7
Sonne – Star and centre of the → solar system.

supply [səˈplaɪ], p. 53
Versorgung – Provision, stock, or store of food or other things necessary for living.

supply company [səˈplaɪ ˈkʌmp(ə)ni], p. 51
Zulieferfirma – → Company producing → components for the → final assembly.

surface [ˈsɜː(r)fɪs], p. 17
Oberfläche – Border between the → Earth's lithosphere and atmosphere.

T

temperature [ˈtemprɪtʃə(r)], p. 23
Temperatur – The measurement in degrees of how hot or cold a thing or a place is.

temperature range
[ˈtemprɪtʃə(r) reɪndʒ], p. 39
Temperaturbereich – The difference between the high and low → temperatures measured over a certain period of time (day, year).

tertiary sector [ˈtɜː(r)ʃəri ˈsektə(r)], p. 49
Tertiärer Sektor – Sector of an economy concerned with the sale and use of economic goods and services.

thermometer [θə(r)ˈmɒmɪtə(r)], p. 25
Thermometer – Shows the current temperature.

tidal energy [ˈtaɪd(ə)l ˈenə(r)dʒi], p. 47
Gezeitenenergie – Sustainable energy which uses the water from the tides to produce → hydroelectric energy.

tilt [tɪlt], p. 15, 21
Neigung, Neigungswinkel – The → Earth's axis is not vertical. It is oblique with an angle of 23.5°.

time difference [taɪm ˈdɪfrəns], p. 19
Zeitunterschied, Zeitverschiebung – Number of hours between places in two → time zones.

time zone [taɪm zəʊn], p. 19
Zeitzone – Division of the → Earth, usually of 15° longitude. There are 24 such divisions within which the mean time of the central → meridian represents the time for the whole time zone.

tourism [ˈtʊərɪz(ə)m], p. 57
Tourismus – Travel for recreational, leisure, family or business purposes.

tourist attraction [ˈtʊərɪst əˈtrækʃ(ə)n], p. 55
Touristenattraktion – Reason why many people visit this place during their holidays. Also the place of this attraction.

tourist industry [ˈtʊərɪst ˈɪndəstri], p. 59, 61
Touristikbranche – People, activities, and organisations involved in providing services for people on holiday.

transitional climate [trænˈzɪʃ(ə)nəl ˈklaɪmət], p. 39
Übergangsklima – → Climate between → maritime and → continental climate in Europe.

travel [ˈtræv(ə)l], p. 53
Reise – Tour or journey.

travel agency [ˈtræv(ə)l ˈeɪdʒ(ə)nsi], p. 57
Reisebüro – Bureau that arranges and negotiates flights, holidays, etc., for holiday makers.

tropical rainforest [ˈtrɒpɪk(ə)l ˈreɪnˌfɒrɪst], p. 27
Tropischer Regenwald – Evergreen vegetation zone, which is a distinctly layered rainforest close to the → Equator.

U

upland [ˈʌplənd], p. 33
Hochland – High lying area of the → Earth with hills and mountains.

urban area [ˈɜː(r)bən ˈeəriə], p. 55
Städtischer Raum – A built up area related to a → city or a densely populated area.

V

vegetation [ˌvedʒəˈteɪʃ(ə)n], p. 27
Vegetation – The generic term for the → Earth's plant life.

vertical rays [ˈvɜː(r)tɪk(ə)l reɪz], p. 21
senkrecht, vertikal einfallende Strahlen – Sun rays that reach the → Earth at an angle of 90°.

W

wave energy [weɪv ˈenə(r)dʒi], p. 47
Wellenenergie – Sustainable energy from ocean surface waves, and the capture of that energy to do useful work.

weather [ˈweðə(r)], p. 23
Wetter – The interaction of the atmospheric elements → precipitation, → temperature, humidity, atmospheric pressure, cloud cover, and wind over a short period of time and at any place.

weather elements [ˈweðə(r) ˈelɪmənts], p. 23
Wetterelemente – Atmospheric elements such as → precipitation, → temperature, humidity, atmospheric pressure, and cloud cover.

weather station [ˈweðə(r) ˈsteɪʃ(ə)n], p. 25
Wetterstation – A place where weather conditions → precipitation, → temperature, wind speed, wind direction, cloud cover and air pressure are studied and recorded.

wind energy [wɪnd ˈenə(r)dʒi], p. 47
Windenergie – Sustainable energy from the conversion of wind into a more useful form of energy, like electricity.

wind speed [wɪnd spiːd], p. 25
Windstärke – Measurement of how strongly the wind blows.

windsock [ˈwɪndˌsɒk], p. 25
Windsack – A fabric tube, open at both ends, that hangs at the top of a pole to show the direction of the wind.

working day [ˈwɜː(r)kːɪŋ ˈdeɪˌ], p. 53
Werktag – Days on which people spend most of their time at work to earn money.

Mithilfe der Tondateien kannst du dir anhören, wie die Key terms ausgesprochen werden. Nutze hierzu wahlweise den Internetlink oder den QR-Code für das Smartphone:

www.westermann.de/ links/114030

Phonetic symbols							
Vowels		*Dipthongs*		*Consonants*			
ɑː	arm	i	happy	aɪ	eye	ŋ	song	ð	these
ʌ	but	iː	easy	aʊ	our	r	red	θ	bathroom
e	desk	ɒ	orange	eə	air	s	sister	v	very
ə	an	ɔː	all	eɪ	take	z	zebra	w	what
ɜː	bird	ʊ	look	ɪə	here	ʒ	television	*Stress*	
æ	apple	u	January	ɔɪ	boy	dʒ	sausage	ˈ	Main stress in a word
ɪ	in	uː	boot	əʊ	go	ʃ	fresh	ˌ	Secondary stress in a word coming before the main stress.
				ʊə	your	tʃ	child		

Sources

|A1PIX - Your Photo Today, Ottobrunn: SAT 32.1. |agrar-press, Koblenz: 42.1. |Airbus, Hamburg: 50.1, 51.1, 51.2, 51.3, 51.4. |Alamy Stock Photo, Abingdon/Oxfordshire: David R. Frazier Photolibrary, Inc. 57.3. |Alamy Stock Photo (RMB), Abingdon/Oxfordshire: age fotostock 49.4; Arch White 55.3; Kreder, Katja 57.4; LatitudeStock 61.4; Loop Images LTD 55.6; Michael Kemp 23.1; VIEW Pictures Ltd/Huflon and Crow 49.5; Yvette Cardozo 56.3. |Alpine Coaster Imst, Imst: Gerhard Berger 59.1. |Appleby, Steven, London: 52.4, 53.3, 55.1, 55.4. |Astrofoto, Sörth: 6.1, 7.1, 14.2. |BASF Corporate History, Ludwigshafen: 49.1. |Betz, Prevorst: 59.2, 59.3. |CLAAS KGaA mbh, Harsewinkel: 43.1. |Conrad Electronic, Hirschau: 25.3. |Diercke Globus online: 26.1. |DLR Deutsches Zentrum für Luft- und Raumfahrt, Weßling, OT Oberpfaffenhofen: 3.2, 16.2. |dreamstime.com, Brentwood: Pat Olson 16.1; Paulpmp 23.2; Steve Allen 27.1; Tomas1111 49.3. |Feldhaus, Hans-Jürgen, Münster: 69.1. |Fotex Medien Agentur GmbH, Hamburg: MLP 56.1. |fotolia.com, New York: AKhodi 36.2; asife 33.3; Bianka Hagge 38.2; Ertl, Johann 26.3, 83.1; Gessler 33.2; grafikplusfoto 12.1; Jargstorff, Wolfgang 41.1; Kaarsten 52.3, 55.5; Light Impression 46.2, 47.1; moonrun 37.3; Reinartz, Petra 42.2; reises 32.2; Rhombur 18.1; Schnell, Roland 25.1; Somwaya 12.3; Thorsten Schier 42.5; © styleuneed 14.1. |Fraport AG, Frankfurt/Main: Stefan Rebscher 37.2. |Fremdenverkehrsamt Malta, Frankfurt/Main: 61.1. |Gampe, Corinna: 46.1, 47.2. |Getty Images, München: Dave G. Houser 38.3; Lisa Wiltse/Sydney Morning Herald/Fairfax Media 13.2; Sean Caffrey 52.1; Sylvain Sonnet Titel; Tim Graham 13.1. |Google Earth: 52.2. |Google Maps / Street View: 53.4. |Hofemeister, Uwe, Diepholz: 22.1, 22.2, 23.4. |Hundertmark, Verena, Köln: 23.3. |Interfoto, München: imagebroker/Jochen Tack 57.2. |iStockphoto.com, Calgary: Albert_Karimov 48.4; catalby 24.1; duncan1890 33.4; EdStock 48.1; intst 38.1; ranplett 26.2; rotofrank 20.1, 20.2, 20.3, 20.4. |laif, Köln: Gläscher, Jörg 16.4; Pierre BESSARD/REA 57.1. |Landesmedienzentrum Baden-Württemberg, Stuttgart: 33.1. |Lothian Buses Plc, Edinburgh: 53.2. |mauritius images GmbH, Mittenwald: ib/Jochen Tack 56.2; imagebroker/allesfoto.com 8.1. |NASA, Washington: 3.1, 10.1; NSSDC Photo Gallery 4.1. |PantherMedia GmbH (panthermedia.net), München: Christophe Kajzar 19.3; Dudko, Ann 58.1; Iakov Filimonov 61.2; Magdalena Ascough 19.2. |Picture-Alliance GmbH, Frankfurt a.M.: ANP Lex van Lieshout 41.2; chromorange/Yuri Arcurs 19.1; dpa-Zentralbild/euroluftbild.de/Clemens, Bernd 44.1; dpa-Zentralbild/Pleul, Patrick 36.1; dpa-Zentralbild/Wüstneck, Bernd 43.2; dpa/Carstensen, Jörg 37.1; dpa/DWD 25.4; dpa/epa Sergey Dolzhenko 38.4; dpa/epa/Graham Stuart 55.2; dpa/Grubitzsch, Waltraud 49.2; Photoshot 48.2; ZB/Büttner, Jens 48.3; ZB/Förster, Peter 43.3; ZUMA Press/mr7 45.1. |Reischauer, Dirk, Hannover: 40.1, 40.2, 42.4, 43.4, 53.1, 54.1, 54.2. |Seipelt, Andrea, Vechelde: 32.3. |Shutterstock.com, New York: Balazik, Robert F. 15.1. |Stadler, Katrin, Landshut: 25.2. |stock.adobe.com, Dublin: suzbah 42.3. |Tegen, Hans, Hambühren: 24.2. |VII Photo Agency, Paris: 12.2. |Visum Foto GmbH, München: A. Vossberg 61.3. |Wendorf, Monika, Hannover: 16.3. |World Sunlight Map/www.die.net/earth: 19.4.

Different Types of Numbers

1. Reading and writing numbers

.	**point** (for decimals, e.g. 2.54). See decimals.
,	Use a comma or a blank for groups of three numbers. (Do not read commas.) See below.
0	**zero**, "0", **nought** (UK)
1–10	In a text write **one** to **ten** as words.
>10	In a text write numbers **larger than** 10 as numbers, e.g. "56", not "fifty-six".
123	a/one **hundred** (and) twenty-three
234	two **hundred** (and) thirty-four
5,678 (5 678)	five **thousand** six hundred (and) seventy-eight
93,000,000	ninety-three **million**
6,000,000,000	six **billion** (milliard = UK old form)

2. Different types of numbers

Ordinal numbers

1st	first	7th	seventh
2nd	second	8th	eighth
3rd	third	9th	ninth
4th	fourth	10th	tenth
5th	fifth	11th	eleventh
6th	sixth	12th	twelfth

Fractions

Fraction	We say …	Decimal	Per cent
1/2	a/one half (of) / one out of two	0.5	50 %
1/3	a/one third (of) / one out of three	0.33	33 1/3 %
1/4	a/one fourth (of) / one out of four	0.25	25 %
1/5	a/one fifth (of) / one out of five	0.2	20 %
1/10	a/one tenth (of) / one out of ten	0.1	10 %
1/20	a/one twentieth (of) / one out of twenty	0.05	5 %
1/100	a/one hundredth (of) / one out of a/one hundred	0.01	1 %

Decimals

0.5	(zero) **point** five
3.14 (π)	three **point** one four (pi)

Powers / Exponents

10^2	ten **squared** / ten **to the power of** two / ten **to the** second	100
10^3	ten **to the power of** three / ten **to the** third	1000

The Earth is 93×10^6 miles from the sun.
(ninety-three **times ten to the sixth**) – 93 million –

3. Arithmetic

= Proportions

=	is, is **equal to**, equals	≠	is **unequal to**, is **not equal to**
>	is **more**, is **larger than**	<	is **less**, is **fewer**, is **smaller than**
4:1	four **to** one	4 x	four **times as large as**

+ Addition → Sum

12	+	4	=	16
Twelve	plus	four	equals	sixteen.

– Subtraction → Difference

12	–	4	=	8
Twelve	minus	four	equals	eight.

X Multiplication → Product

12	x	4	=	48
Twelve	times, multiplied by	four	equals	forty-eight.

÷ Division → Quotient

12	÷ /	4	=	3
Twelve	divided by	four	equals	three.

4. Geometry

	parallel lines
90°	**right angle** = 90° A right angle has got ninety **degrees**.
(circle)	**circle** A circle is **round** or **circular**. It has got a **middle point (M)**. The line from the middle point to the circle wall is the **radius (r)**. The line from one side of the circle through the middle point to the other side is the **diameter (d)**.
x≠y	**rectangle** A rectangle is **rectangular**. It has got two parallel equal sides on two sides at right angles.
x=y	**square** A square is **square**. It has got four equal parallel sides at right angles.
△	**triangle** A triangle is **triangular**. It has got three sides.

3-d figures

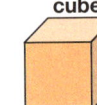
cube

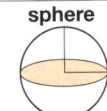
sphere

5. Time

1 minute	= 60 seconds	
60 minutes	= 1 hour	2006
24 hours	= 1 day	two thousand (and) six
365 ¼ days	= 1 year	twenty "o" six
100 years	= 1 century	